The Bill of Rights
Evolution of Personal Liberties

&

Teachers Guide
A Supplemental Teaching Unit
from the Records of the National Archives

NATIONAL
ARCHIVES

National Archives Trust Fund Board
National Archives and Records Administration

A B C   C L I O

ABC – CLIO, Inc
130 Cremona Drive, P.O. Box 1911
Santa Barbara, CA 93116-1911
ISBN 1-57607-779-9

Other Units in this Series:

The Constitution: Evolution of a Government

The United States Expands West: 1785-1842

Westward Expansion: 1842-1912

The Civil War: Soldiers and Civilians

The Progressive Years: 1898-1917

World War I: The Home Front

The 1920's

The Great Depression and The New Deal

World War II: The Home Front

The United States At War: 1944

The Truman Years: 1945-1953

Peace and Prosperity: 1953-1961

but decrees that all born or naturalized in the land are equal before the law. If a State be tolerated in shutting the colored man out of the public schools it might with equal reason be allowed to deny to him the right to testify or vote.

4. We would remind our Rulers that in those dark days when a gigantic Rebellion threatened the national life, the colored men of Tennessee, so loved liberty, that while yet slaves and with no promise even of personal freedom for their race, they rushed by thousands into the Federal armies. We do not complain that the disabilities of the men we then fought, are removed, but we confess ourselves unable to understand on what principle of equity or expediency it is that our own disabilities are allowed to remain. We do not question the policy of the General Government being magnanimous to its enemies, but we must doubt the wisdom of its tolerating States in visiting insult and injury upon its friends.

5. We urge our Petition with the more of assurance since all we claim was pledged us in both of the Party Platforms of 1872 - platforms voted upon by more than six millions of American freemen. We ask respectfully but with earnestness, and persistently, that the pledge thus solemnly given by the nation be redeemed.

Names

Anthony Coster.
Geo. F. Warson.
Moses Brown
Elyze Parks
Geo. Calaway.
Scott Penston
Geo Christmas.

Names

Table of Contents

Foreword

In its efforts to make the historical records of the federal government available nationally, the National Archives began a program in 1970 to introduce these vast resources to secondary school students. School classes visiting the National Archives in Washington were given the opportunity to examine and interpret original sources as historians use them. Teachers and students responded enthusiastically and encouraged the development of a series of supplemental teaching units.

The Bill of Rights: Evolution of Personal Liberties is the tenth unit in the series. It, like those that have preceded and will follow, is intended to bring you and your students the excitement and satisfaction of working with primary sources and to enhance your instructional program.

DON W. WILSON
Archivist of the United States
1989

...to bring you and your students the excitement and satisfaction of working with primary sources and to enhance your instructional program.

Preface

- This unit is made up of 10 exercises.

- Each exercise includes reproductions of documents from the National Archives and suggests classroom activities based on these documents.

The Bill of Rights: Evolution of Personal Liberties is a teaching unit designed to supplement your students' study of the Bill of Rights. The unit is made up of 10 exercises. Each exercise includes reproductions of documents from the National Archives and suggests classroom activities based on these documents. The documents include official correspondence, petitions, photographs, posters, newspapers, maps, and court decisions. Students practice the historian's skills as they complete exercises, using these documents to gather information, identify points of view, evaluate evidence, form hypotheses, and draw conclusions.

The documents in this unit do not reflect every topic usually included in a history or government textbook. In some instances the federal government had no interest in or authority over a given event and therefore created no records on it. In other cases documents in the National Archives on several historic topics proved to be difficult to use in the classroom due to problems with legibility and length. Many textbooks treat the post-Revolutionary period as a whole, so teachers may find it useful to use the companion unit, *The Constitution: Evolution of a Government*, along with this one.

The Bill of Rights: Evolution of Personal Liberties is useful in the government classroom as well as the history classroom. Activities included in all exercises are designed for use by government and civics teachers. Documents 1, 4, 5, 7, 12, 14, 15, 26, 27, 29, 33, and 46 were generated by the legislative branch. The executive branch created documents 9, 17, 21, 22, 28, 32, and 34. Documents from the judicial branch include 8, 11, 13, 19, 20, 23, 24, 25, 30, 31, and 35. The citizens and the states generated the remaining documents, 2, 3, 6, 10, 16, 18, 36, 37, 38, 39, 40, 41, 42, 43, 44, and 45.

National Archives education specialists Jean M. West and Wynell Burroughs Schamel and education branch chief Elsie Freeman Finch developed this publication. We are pleased to issue a revised and updated set of these documentary teaching materials.

WYNELL B. SCHAMEL
LEE ANN POTTER
Education Specialists
2001

The Bill of Rights: Evolution of Personal Liberties is a teaching unit designed to supplement your students' study of the Bill of Rights.

Acknowledgments

Many people helped in the original production of this unit. They included National Archives staff members Linda Ebben, Dane Hartgrove, Calvin Jefferson, Chauncey Jessup, Michael Knapp, Mary Walton Livingston, Mary Ronan, Aloha South, Reggie Washington, and Marc Wolfe.

Jeri-Lynn Gatto, a classroom teacher in Mays Landing, NJ; Tom Gray, a classroom teacher in De Ruyter, NY; James Percoco, a classroom teacher in Fairfax County, VA; and other social studies teachers reviewed elements of this unit. Their reactions and comments shaped and improved the document selection and the teaching exercises.

Karen Berlin, a National Archives volunteer, assisted in the development of the time line and reviewed the eighth exercise. Linda N. Brown, Assistant Archivist of the Office of Public Programs; Dane Hartgrove, archivist in the Diplomatic Branch; Edith James, Director of the Exhibits and Educational Programs Division; and Edward O'Brien, Co-Director of the National Institute for Citizen Education in the Law, reviewed the unit for historical content. Greg Bradsher, of the Planning and Policy Evaluation Branch, reviewed the first three exercises, and JoAnn Williamson, of the Military Records Branch, reviewed the ninth exercise for accuracy. [Positions held at the time of original publication.]

Special thanks go to Ron Lucero of the National Archives Volunteer Association for his assistance throughout this project. He researched a score of landmark cases in the Supreme Court records and scanned numerous rolls of microfilmed records of the Continental Congress at the outset. Later on, he helped to develop the annotated bibliography and table of cases. Finally, he lent his legal expertise to review the package for accuracy.

During the republication process, we were ably assisted by George Mason University intern Adam Jevec; volunteers, Elizabeth S. Lourie, Jane Douma Pearson, and Donald Alderson; and National Archives staff members Michael Hussey, A.J. Daverede, Patrick Osborn, Amy Patterson, Kate Flaherty, Donald Roe, and Charles Mayn.

$\mathcal{P}$ublisher's Note

Primary source documents have long been a cornerstone of ABC-CLIO's commitment to producing high-quality, learner-centered history and social studies resources. When our nation's students have the opportunity to interact with the undiluted artifacts of the past, they can better understand the breadth of the human experience and the present state of affairs.

It is with great enthusiasm that we celebrate the release of this series of teaching units designed in partnership with the National Archives—materials that we hope will bring historical context and deeper knowledge to U.S. middle and high school students. Each unit has been revised and updated, including new bibliographic references. Each teaching unit has been correlated to the curriculum standards for the teaching of social studies and history developed by the National Council for the Social Studies and the National Center for History in the Schools.

For more effective use of these teaching units in the classroom, each booklet is accompanied by an interactive CD-ROM which includes exercise worksheets, digital images of original documents, and, for four titles, sound recordings. A videocassette of motion pictures accompanies the teaching unit *The United States At War: 1944*. For those who would like to order facsimiles of primary source documents in their original sizes, or additional titles in this series, we have included an order form to make it easy for you to do so.

The mission of the National Archives is "to ensure ready access to the essential evidence that documents the rights of American citizens, the actions of Federal officials, and the national experience."

These units go a long way toward fulfilling that mission, helping the next generation of American citizens develop a clear understanding of the nation's past and a firm grasp of the role of the individual in guiding the nation's future. ABC-CLIO is honored to be part of this process.

BECKY SNYDER
Publisher & Vice President
ABC-CLIO Schools

The mission of the National Archives is "to ensure ready access to the essential evidence that documents the rights of American citizens, the actions of Federal officials, and the national experience."

Teaching With Documents Curriculum Standards Correlations

The National Council for the Social Studies and the National Center for History in the Schools have developed a set of comprehensive curriculum standards for the teaching of social studies and history. Take a look at how thoroughly the Teaching With Documents series supports the curriculum.

National Council for the Social Studies

Time Period	CULTURE	TIME, CONTINUITY & CHANGE	PEOPLE, PLACES & ENVIRONMENT	INDIVIDUAL DEVELOPMENT & IDENTITY	INDIVIDUALS, GROUPS & INSTITUTIONS	POWER, AUTHORITY & GOVERNANCE	PRODUCTION, DISTRIBUTION & CONSUMPTION	SCIENCE, TECHNOLOGY & SOCIETY	GLOBAL CONNECTIONS	CIVIC IDEALS & PRACTICES
The Constitution: Evolution of a Government	●	●	●	●	●	●	●		●	●
The Bill of Rights: Evolution of Personal Liberties		●	●	●	●	●				●
The United States Expands West: 1785–1842	●	●	●	●	●	●	●		●	
Westward Expansion: 1842–1912	●		●	●	●	●	●			
The Civil War: Soldiers and Civilians			●	●	●	●		●		
The Progressive Years: 1898–1917			●		●	●	●		●	
World War I: The Home Front			●	●			●			
The 1920's	●		●	●	●	●		●		●
The Great Depression and The New Deal World			●	●	●	●	●			
War II: The Home Front	●		●							
The United States At War: 1944		●			●			●	●	●
The Truman Years: 1945–1953					●	●	●	●	●	
Peace and Prosperity: 1953–1961	●			●	●	●		●	●	

National Center for History in the Schools

Time Period	CHRONOLOGICAL THINKING	HISTORICAL COMPREHENSION	HISTORICAL ANALYSIS & INTERPRETATION	HISTORICAL RESEARCH CAPABILITIES	HISTORICAL ISSUES-ANALYSIS & DECISION-MAKING
The Constitution: Evolution of a Government	●	●	●	●	●
The Bill of Rights: Evolution of Personal Liberties	●	●	●	●	●
The United States Expands West: 1785–1842	●	●	●	●	●
Westward Expansion: 1842–1912	●	●	●	●	●
The Civil War: Soldiers and Civilians	●	●	●	●	●
The Progressive Years: 1898–1917	●	●	●	●	●
World War I: The Home Front	●	●	●	●	●
The 1920's	●	●	●	●	●
The Great Depression and The New Deal World	●	●	●	●	●
War II: The Home Front	●	●	●	●	●
The United States At War: 1944	●	●	●	●	●
The Truman Years: 1945–1953	●	●	●	●	●
Peace and Prosperity: 1953–1961	●	●	●	●	●

Introduction

This unit contains two elements: 1) a book, which contains a teachers guide and a set of reproductions of print documents, and 2) a CD-ROM, which contains the exercise worksheets from the teachers guide and a set of reproductions of documents in electronic format. In selecting the documents, we applied three standards. First, the documents must be entirely from the holdings of the National Archives and must reflect the actions of the federal government or citizens' responses to those actions. Second, each document must be typical of the hundreds of records of its kind relating to its particular topic. Third, the documents must be legible and potentially useful for vocabulary development. In selecting documents we tried to choose those having appeal to young people.

Objectives

We have provided an outline of the general objectives for the unit. You will be able to achieve these objectives by completing several, if not all, of the exercises in the unit. Because each exercise aims to develop skills defined in the general objectives, you may be selective and still develop those skills. In addition, each exercise has its own specific objectives.

UNIT CONTAINS:

◆ **1)** a book, which contains a teachers guide and a set of reproductions of print documents, and

◆ **2)** a CD-ROM, which contains the exercise worksheets from the teachers guide and a set of reproductions of documents in electronic format.

Outline

This unit on the evolution of the Bill of Rights has three sections. The first section examines the history of the writing of the Bill of Rights, the second the evolution of the Bill of Rights since its adoption, and the third the Bill of Rights and the future. The structure and relation of the exercises and documents to these sections are presented in the Outline of Classroom Exercises, p. 4.

List of Documents

The list of documents gives specific information (e.g., date and name of author) and record group number for each document. Records in the National Archives are arranged in record groups. A typical record group (RG) consists of the records created or accumulated by a department, agency, bureau, or other administrative unit of the federal government. Each record group is identified for retrieval purposes by a record group number; for example, RG 107 (Office of the Secretary of War) or RG 267 (Supreme Court). Complete archival citations of all documents are listed in the appendix, p. 67.

Exercise Summary Chart

The chart shows the organization of the 10 exercises. For each exercise the chart outlines the materials needed, the document content, the student activities that are emphasized, and the number of class periods needed. Review the chart carefully and decide which exercises to use based on your objectives for the students, their ability levels, and the content you wish to teach. The exercises may be adapted to fit your objectives and teaching style.

Introductory Exercises

Before starting exercises 1-10, it is important to familiarize students with documents and their importance to the historian who interprets them and writes history from them. We suggest that you direct students to do one or all of the introductory exercises. Introduction to Documents, p. 10, is designed to increase students' awareness of documents in their environment and is suitable for upper elementary and all secondary students. The Historian's Tools, p. 11, is designed to increase students' awareness of the process of analyzing historical information and is most appropriate for students working at or above ninth grade reading level. The Written Document Analysis, p. 13, is designed to help students analyze systematically any written document in this unit. The Photograph Analysis, p. 14, can be used for the same purpose with any of the photographs in the unit. The Poster Analysis, p. 15, can be used to help in the systematic analysis of posters.

Classroom Exercises

This unit contains 10 suggested exercises. Within the explanatory material for each of the exercises, you will find the following information:

- ➤ Note to the teacher
- ➤ Classroom time required
- ➤ Objectives (specific)
- ➤ Materials needed
- ➤ Procedures
- ➤ Student worksheets

You may choose to combine several exercises on a topic within the unit. In some instances a document is used in more than one exercise when appropriate to the skill or content objectives. We encourage you to select and adapt the exercises and documents that best suit your own teaching style.

Ability Levels

As in our other units, we have developed exercises for students of different abilities. For some topics, we have designed two or more procedures, tailored to different student needs. Throughout the unit we have made an effort to provide exercises in which students use a variety of skills, including reading for understanding, interpreting maps and posters, and analyzing legislation and court cases. All lessons have procedures for ability levels two, and three. Procedures begin with strategies designed for level three students, continue with level two strategies, and conclude with level one strategies. Our definition of student ability at each ability level is as follows:

Level One: Good reading skills, ability to organize and interpret information from several sources with minimal direction from teacher, and ability to complete assignments independently.

Level Two: Average reading skills, ability to organize and interpret information from several sources with general direction from teacher, and ability to complete assignments with some assistance from teacher.

Level Three: Limited reading skills, and ability to organize and interpret information from several sources with step-by-step direction from teacher, and ability to complete assignments with close supervision from teacher.

These ability levels are merely guides. We recognize that you will adapt the exercises to suit your students' needs and your own teaching style.

Time Line

A time line is included for use by your students. You may want to reproduce it for each student or display it.

Table of Cases

A table of cases with legal citations is included for use by you or your students to ease research into Supreme Court cases mentioned in this unit.

Bibliography

As students work with the documents, they should be assigned appropriate readings from their text and other secondary sources. They should also be encouraged to use the resources of school and public libraries. To guide them, an annotated bibliography appears at the end of the Teachers Guide.

General Objectives

Upon successfully completing the exercises in this unit, students should be able to demonstrate the following skills using a single document:

➤ Identify factual evidence
➤ Identify points of view (bias and/or prejudice)
➤ Collect, reorder, and weigh the significance of evidence
➤ Develop defensible inferences, conclusions, and generalizations from factual information

Using several documents from this unit, students should be able to:

➤ Analyze the documents to compare and contrast evidence
➤ Evaluate and interpret evidence drawn from the documents

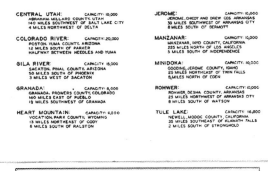

RELOCATION PROJECT SITES

CENTRAL UTAH: CAPACITY: 10,000
ABRAHAM, MILLARD COUNTY, UTAH
140 MILES SOUTHWEST OF SALT LAKE CITY
4 MILES NORTHWEST OF DELTA

COLORADO RIVER: CAPACITY: 20,000
POSTON, YUMA COUNTY, ARIZONA
12 MILES SOUTH OF PARKER
HALFWAY BETWEEN NEEDLES AND YUMA

GILA RIVER: CAPACITY: 15,000
SACATON, PINAL COUNTY, ARIZONA
50 MILES SOUTH OF PHOENIX
3 MILES WEST OF SACATON

GRANADA: CAPACITY: 8,000
GRANADA, PROWERS COUNTY, COLORADO
140 MILES EAST OF PUEBLO
1½ MILES SOUTHWEST OF GRANADA

HEART MOUNTAIN: CAPACITY: 11,000
VOCATION, PARK COUNTY, WYOMING
13 MILES NORTHEAST OF CODY
8 MILES SOUTH OF RALSTON

JEROME: CAPACITY: 10,000
JEROME, CHICOT AND DREW COS, ARKANSAS
30 MILES SOUTHWEST OF ARKANSAS CITY
8 MILES SOUTH OF DERMOTT

MANZANAR: CAPACITY: 10,000
MANZANAR, INYO COUNTY, CALIFORNIA
225 MILES NORTH OF LOS ANGELES
5 MILES SOUTH OF INDEPENDENCE

MINIDOKA: CAPACITY: 10,000
GOODING, JEROME COUNTY, IDAHO
25 MILES NORTHEAST OF TWIN FALLS
8 MILES NORTH OF EDEN

ROHWER: CAPACITY: 10,000
ROHWER, DESHA COUNTY, ARKANSAS
25 MILES NORTHWEST OF ARKANSAS CITY
8 MILES SOUTH OF WATSON

TULE LAKE: CAPACITY: 16,000
NEWELL, MODOC COUNTY, CALIFORNIA
35 MILES SOUTHEAST OF KLAMATH FALLS
2 MILES SOUTH OF STRONGHOLD

◆ WAR RELOCATION PROJECT SITES

FIGURE 21

Outline of Classroom Exercises

The Bill of Rights: Evolution of Personal Liberties

I. The History of the Bill of Rights

    A. Exercise 1: The Revolutionary Background of the Bill of Rights

    B. Exercise 2: Writing and Adopting the Federal Bill of Rights

    C. Exercise 3: The 14th Amendment and Attempts to Nationalize the Bill of Rights

II. The Evolution of the Bill of Rights

    A. Exercise 4: The First Amendment

    B. Exercise 5: The Second Amendment

    C. Exercise 6: Due Process and the Rights of the Accused

    D. Exercise 7: Rights of Minors

    E. Exercise 8: The Internment of Japanese-American Citizens: The Bill of Rights Outside of the Fence and Inside of the Fence

III. The Bill of Rights and the Future

    A. Exercise 9: Individual Rights and the Common Good

    B. Exercise 10: Summary Exercise: The Bill of Rights

List of Documents

Following the identifying information for each document reproduced in the unit, we have given the record group (RG) number in which the original can be found. Should you want copies of these documents or, for other reasons, wish to refer to them in correspondence with us, give the complete archival citation, which is found in the appendix on page 67. **You may duplicate any of the documents in this unit for use with your students.**

Documents in *The Bill of Rights: Evolution of Personal Liberties* are taken from the following record groups: General Records of the U.S. Government (RG 11), United States Postal Service (RG 28), United States Senate (RG 46), Department of Justice (RG 60), Office of the Secretary of War (RG 107), War Relocation Authority (RG 210), U.S. House of Representatives (RG 233), Supreme Court of the United States (RG 267), United States Army Commands (RG 338), and Continental and Confederation Congresses and the Constitutional Convention (RG 360). Additional documents are taken from the holdings of the Lyndon Baines Johnson Presidential Library.

1. Declaration of Rights, October 14, 1774 (RG 360).

2. Resolution of Providence, RI, to ask Congress for money to quarter troops, July 3, 1779 (RG 360).

3. North Carolina's proposed amendments to the Constitution, August 1, 1788 (RG 11).

4. House journal recording the 17 amendments proposed for a bill of rights, August 21, 1789 (RG 233).

5. Enrolled original of the Bill of Rights, September 28, 1789 (RG 11).

6. Virginia Ratification of the Bill of Rights, December 15, 1791 (RG 11).

7. Fourteenth Amendment to the Constitution, June 16, 1866 (RG 11).

8. Petition for a writ of error in the Slaughterhouse cases, May 13, 1870 (RG 267).

9. H.C. Whitley's report to Attorney General George Williams about the Ku Klux Klan, September 29, 1871 (RG 60).

10. Petition for the enforcement of the Fourteenth Amendment, January 19, 1874 (RG 233).

11. Amicus curiae brief of the American Civil Liberties Union in *Everson v. Board of Education of Ewing Township, New Jersey*, November 14, 1946 (RG 267).

12. Resolution submitted by Senator Powell condemning Grant's General Order No. 11, January 5, 1863 (RG 46).

13. Mandate in *West Virginia v. Barnette*, June 14, 1943 (RG 267).

14. Petition for restoration of Thomas Cooper's fine, February 24, 1825 (RG 46).

15. The Espionage Act, June 15, 1917 (RG 11).

16. "Garfield Wastes Coal and Electric Lights," *Los Angeles Daily Times*, November 12, 1917 (RG 60).

17. John O'Brian's letter to U.S. Attorney Hooper Alexander about *The Finished Mystery*, May 15, 1918 (RG 60).

18. Poster, "True Blue," 1919 (RG 28).

19. Samuel Young's letter to the Clerk of the Supreme Court about *Gitlow v. New York*, November 6, 1925 (RG 267).

20. Testimony of John Tinker in *Tinker v. Des Moines*, July 25, 1966 (RG 267).

21. Smothers Brothers' letter to President Johnson, October 31, 1968 (Lyndon Baines Johnson Presidential Library).

22. Lawrence Jones' letter to Senator Warren Magnuson about federal firearms legislation, December 18, 1963 (RG 46).

23. Answer to response to petition for a writ of certiorari in *Gideon v. Wainwright*, April 19, 1962 (RG 267).

24. Affidavit in forma pauperis from *Miranda v. Arizona*, July 13, 1965 (RG 267).

25. Selections from the transcript of record of *Furman v. Georgia*, August 11, 1967, and September 20, 1968 (RG 267).

26. *Legislative Notice* about S. (Senate bill) 1765, February 1, 1984 (RG 46).

27. H. J. Res. (House joint resolution) 184, proposing an amendment to control child labor, December 3, 1923 (RG 11).

28. Proclamation by President Eisenhower of Child Health Day, April 2, 1956 (RG 11).

29. National Defense Education Act, September 2, 1958 (RG 11).

30. Commitment order to state industrial school from the case of *in re Gault*, June 15, 1964 (RG 267).

31. Ralph Evans' letter to Justice Douglas about *Goss v. Lopez*, 1974 (RG 267).

32. Executive Order No. 9066, February 19, 1942 (RG 11).

33. Public Law 503, March 21, 1942 (RG 11).

34. Map, Relocation Project Sites, June 5, 1943 (RG 338).

35. Judgment in *Korematsu v. United States*, December 18, 1944 (RG 267).

36. Petition requesting reconsideration of Japanese-American evacuation, April 15, 1942 (RG 338).

37. Newspaper column, "The Fifth Column On The Coast," by Walter Lippmann, February 12, 1942 (RG 107).

38. Essay, "The Fence," by an evacuee, August 11, 1943 (RG 210).

39. Chart, "Age, Sex and Nativity Composition, Heart Mountain, Wyoming," November 1942 (RG 210).

40. Watercolor of Heart Mountain by Estelle Ishigo, February 19, 1943 (RG 210).

41. Photograph, "Heart Mountain," November 1942 (RG 210).

42. Church journal, *Heart Mountain Buddhist's Digest*, July 7, 1943 (RG 210).

43. Yearbook, Hunt High School *Memoirs*, 1944 (RG 210).

44. Interview with the Student Relocation Counselor of Topaz, UT, April 1944 (RG 210).

45. Advertisement, "Heed Their Rising Voices," March 29, 1960 (RG 267).

46. S. 1160, which became the Freedom of Information Act, October 4, 1965 (RG 46).

Exercise Summary Chart

EXERCISE	NUMBER OF DOCUMENTS	CONTENT	STUDENT ACTIVITIES	NUMBER OF CLASS PERIODS
Introductory Exercises	Variable	Introduction to primary sources	Distinguishing between primary and secondary sources Analyzing written documents, photographs, posters Locating personal documents	variable
1. The Revolutionary Background of the Bill of Rights Documents 1-2 Worksheet 1	2	Continental Congress demands the rights of Englishmen Disapproval of quartering troops	Analyzing documents and drawing conclusions	1
2. Writing and Adopting the Federal Bill of Rights Documents 3-6 Worksheet 2	4	The Bill of Rights as drafted and approved	Examining the process of writing the Bill of Rights Examining the content of the Bill of Rights Comparing and contrasting early and final versions of a document Working in groups	2
3. The 14th Amendment and Attempts to Nationalize the Bill of Rights Documents 7-10 Worksheet 3	4	The Fourteenth Amendment The amendment process and other methods of change	Brainstorming Analyzing and drawing conclusions from a group of documents Gathering information Examining the amendment process and other methods of change	2
4. The First Amendment Documents 11-21, 36 Worksheet 4 Poster Analysis worksheet Written Document Analysis worksheet	11	First Amendment rights of religion, expression, and petition	Analyzing and drawing conclusions from a group of documents about the scope of the First Amendment Interpreting a poster Developing and applying vocabulary	2
5. The Second Amendment Document 22	2	The right to bear arms Federal decision-making techniques	Identifying methods for influencing public policy Tracing interpretations of the Second Amendment Using creative writing skills to frame a persuasive statement	1

EXERCISE	NUMBER OF DOCUMENTS	CONTENT	STUDENT ACTIVITIES	NUMBER OF CLASS PERIODS
6. Due Process and the Rights of the Accused Documents 23-26 Worksheets 5 and 6 Written Document Analysis worksheet	4	Evolution of the incorporation of the Fifth and Sixth Amendment rights of the accused through the Fourteenth Amendment	Developing vocabulary of legal terms Identifying rights of the accused Examining the evolution of federal protection of the accused Collecting and interpreting statistical information Writing creatively to compose an interior monologue	2-3
7. Rights of Minors Documents 27-31 Written Document Analysis worksheet	5	Rights of minors The Ninth Amendment	Analyzing documents and drawing conclusions Researching from school records Working in groups	1-2
8. The Internment of Japanese-American Citizens Documents 32-44 Worksheet 7 Photograph Analysis worksheet	13	Impact of the internment of Japanese-Americans on the Bill of Rights	Appraising documents for their historical value Analyzing a photograph Creative writing Evaluating the vigor of the Bill of Rights based on documentary evidence	2
9. Individual Rights and the Common Good Documents 45-46	2	Conflicts in rights Emerging rights of information and privacy	Debating points of view Researching from community sources Analyzing and evaluating the rights to information and privacy Letter writing	2-3
10. Summary Exercise: The Bill of Rights Documents 1-46	46	Interrelationships of all the unit documents	Comparing and contrasting the Bill of Rights with other countries' rights Projecting future trends for the Bill of Rights Researching related topics	1 term

Introductory Exercises

These exercises introduce students to the general objectives of the unit. They focus students' attention on documents and their importance to historians, who interpret and record the past. We encourage you to use one or more of them as opening exercises for this unit.

Introduction to Documents

The Introduction to Documents worksheet is designed to increase students' awareness of documents in their environment and to make students more comfortable and sensitive to working with documents. It focuses on the availability of personal documents, the types of information found therein, and the informal creation and retention of documents in the students' lives. In section 1, students locate a personal document. In section 2, they present the document to the class, summarizing key information contained in the document. Finally, in section 3, the class considers possible reasons for the creation and retention of personal documents. This exercise is a basic introduction to personal documents that should precede study of more formal documents.

The Historian's Tools

The Historian's Tools worksheet is designed to increase students' awareness of the process of analyzing historical information. It focuses on both the nature of the process of analyzing historical information and those factors that influence the historian's analysis of evidence. The worksheet includes specific questions on distinctions between primary and secondary sources, the reliability of those sources, and the influence of bias, point of view, and perspective on the historian's interpretation.

Students do not analyze documents to complete this worksheet as they do in other exercises in the unit. Class discussion, however, is essential to helping students understand the issues raised by the worksheet because there are many ways to answer the questions. In your discussion, stress the fact that reliability is affected by the events surrounding the creation of the document and the purposes for which the document is being evaluated. For this reason it is essential to set documents in their historical context. Also, remind students that primary sources are not necessarily more reliable than well-researched secondary sources. You may wish to assign the worksheet as homework and discuss it with students in class.

Written Document Analysis

The Written Document Analysis worksheet helps students to analyze systematically any written document in this unit. In sections 1-5 of the worksheet, students locate basic details within the document. In section 6, students analyze the document more critically as they complete items A-E. There are many possible correct answers to section 6, A-E. We suggest you use one of documents 10, 14, 23-31, or 36 with this worksheet.

Photograph Analysis

The Photograph Analysis worksheet helps students to identify systematically the historical evidence within photographs. It is designed to improve students' ability to use photographs as historical documents. It can be used specifically with exercise 8.

Poster Analysis

The Poster Analysis worksheet helps students to analyze systematically the historical evidence in posters. It is designed to improve students' ability to analyze the visual and written information contained in posters. It can be used specifically with exercise 4.

Introduction to Documents

Worksheet

1. This evening, with the help of a family member or an adult who is close to you, look through the souvenirs of your life that have been saved as you have grown. For example, these might include a photograph, a letter, a diary, a newspaper clipping, a birth certificate, a report card, or a library or social security card. Select one item to bring into class that you are willing to share with your classmates and teacher.

2. During your turn in class, present your document providing the following information:

   a. What type of document is this?

   b. What is the date of the document?

   c. Who created the document?

   d. How does the document relate to you?

3. Consider, for your document and the documents of your classmates, responses to the following questions:

   a. What does the existence of this document say about whoever created it?

   b. What does the existence of this document say about whoever saved it?

   c. What does the existence of this document say about American life in this era?

Designed and developed by the education staff of the National Archives and Records Administration, Washington, DC 20408.

The Historian's Tools

Worksheet

1. If you were writing a chapter in your textbook about the Bill of Rights, list three things you would like to know about that subject.

   1. _____

   2. _____

   3. _____

2. Where might you look to find information about the three topics you listed in #1?

Topic	**Source of Information**
_____	_____
_____	_____
_____	_____

3. Historians classify sources of information as **PRIMARY** or **SECONDARY**. Primary sources are those created by people who actually saw or participated in an event and recorded that event or their reactions to it immediately after the event. Secondary sources are those created by someone either not present when that event occurred or removed from it by time. Classify the sources of information you listed in #2 as either primary or secondary by placing a **P** or **S** next to your answers in #2. Reconsider the sources you would use to find information about the Bill of Rights; list three more here:

   1. _____

   2. _____

   3. _____

4. Some sources of historical information are viewed as more **RELIABLE** than others, though all of them may be useful. Factors such as bias, self interest, physical distance, and faulty memory affect the reliability of a source. Below is a list of sources of information about the personal liberties of Japanese-American citizens in Heart Mountain, WY, relocation camp. Rate the reliability of each source on a numerical scale in which 1 is reliable and 5 very unreliable. Be able to support your ratings.

   A. The quarterly report produced by the camp council for the War Relocation Authority in February 1943.   1   2   3   4   5

   B. A summary of an interview with a student relocation counselor at Heart Mountain in April 1944.   1   2   3   4   5

C. A newspaper article written by a news
   reporter the day after visiting Heart Mountain.   1   2   3   4   5

D. A transcript of an interview conducted with a
   former evacuee 8 years after leaving Heart Mountain. 1   2   3   4   5

E. A U.S. history high school textbook description
   of the Japanese American internment during the
   Second World War.   1   2   3   4   5

F. A description in an encyclopedia of the
   internment of Japanese American citizens.   1   2   3   4   5

5. What personal and social factors might influence historians as they write about people and
events of the past?

_____

_____

_____

6. What personal and social factors influence *you* as you read historical accounts of people
and events?

_____

_____

_____

Designed and developed by the education staff of the National Archives and Records Administration, Washington, DC 20408.

Written Document Analysis

Worksheet

1. Type of Document (Check one):
   _____ Newspaper   _____ Map   _____ Advertisement
   _____ Letter   _____ Telegram   _____ Congressional record
   _____ Patent   _____ Press release   _____ Census report
   _____ Memorandum   _____ Report   _____ Other

2. Unique Physical Qualities of the Document (check one or more):
   _____ Interesting letterhead   _____ Notations
   _____ Handwritten   _____ "RECEIVED" stamp
   _____ Typed   _____ Other
   _____ Seals

3. Date(s) of Document: _____

4. Author (or creator) of the Document: _____

   Position (Title): _____

5. For What Audience was the Document Written? _____

6. Document Information (There are many possible ways to answer A-E.)

   A. List three things the author said that you think are important:

      1. _____

      2. _____

      3. _____

   B. Why do you think this document was written?

      _____

      _____

   C. What evidence in the document helps you to know why it was written?
      Quote from the document.

      _____

      _____

   D. List two things the document tells you about life in the United States
      at the time it was written:

      1. _____

      2. _____

   E. Write a question to the author that is left unanswered by the document:

      _____

      _____

Designed and developed by the education staff of the National Archives and Records Administration, Washington, DC 20408.

Photograph Analysis

Worksheet

Step 1. Observation

A. Study the photograph for 2 minutes. Form an overall impression of the photograph and then examine individual items. Next, divide the photo into quadrants and study each section to see what new details become visible.

B. Use the chart below to list people, objects, and activities in the photograph.

PEOPLE	OBJECTS	ACTIVITIES
_____	_____	_____
_____	_____	_____
_____	_____	_____
_____	_____	_____
_____	_____	_____
_____	_____	_____

Step 2. Inference

Based on what you have observed above, list three things you might infer from this photograph:

1. _____

2. _____

3. _____

Step 3. Questions

A. What questions does this photograph raise in your mind?

_____

_____

B. Where could you find answers to them?

_____

_____

Designed and developed by the education staff of the National Archives and Records Administration, Washington, DC 20408.

Poster Analysis

Worksheet

1. What are the main colors used in the poster?

   _____

   _____

2. What symbols (if any) are used in the poster?

   _____

   _____

3. If a symbol is used, is it

   _____

   _____

   a. clear (easy to interpret)?

   _____

   _____

   b. memorable?

   _____

   _____

   c. dramatic?

   _____

   _____

4. Are the messages in the poster more visual or verbal?

   _____

   _____

5. Who do you think is the intended audience for the poster?

   _____

   _____

6. What does the government hope that the audience will do?

   _____

   _____

7. What purpose(s) of government are served by the poster?

   _____

   _____

8. The most effective posters use symbols that are unusual, simple, and direct. Is this an effective poster?

   _____

   _____

Designed and developed by the education staff of the National Archives and Records Administration, Washington, DC 20408.

Exercise 1
The Revolutionary Background of the Bill of Rights

Note to the Teacher:

The Bill of Rights arose largely from the experiences of American colonists with British government, but it differed from its closest British counterparts. As British subjects, the colonists claimed the traditional rights of Englishmen extending back to the Middle Ages and exemplified in Magna Carta. In 1215, Magna Carta affirmed the right to protection of life, liberty, and property from capricious government action, specifically guaranteeing trial by jury and the writ of habeas corpus. The 1628 English Petition of Right forbade quartering troops without the consent of the proprietor and restated the right to due process of law.

By 1689, common law and statute law were committed to paper to reinforce these traditional freedoms. Consequently, the English Bill of Rights was adopted to provide safeguards against royal abuses including excessive bails and fines, cruel and unusual punishment, and maintaining a standing army in peacetime. It also affirmed the right to petition and the right of Protestants to bear arms. Although it inspired language used in the American Bill of Rights, the English bill was less comprehensive, notably ignoring rights to free speech, press, and religion. And because it was an act of Parliament, it was subject to repeal by a parliamentary majority at any time.

From the time the colonies were settled and chartered until the eve of the Revolutionary War, colonial legislatures passed acts and promulgated compacts that identified and guaranteed most personal liberties. With the end of the French and Indian War, however, relations between Great Britain and her colonies deteriorated, in part because colonists saw their rights being infringed upon or violated by agents of the Crown. By the time the First Continental Congress met at Carpenters' Hall in Philadelphia on September 5, 1774, colonial leaders had reached the consensus that a declaration of rights would be the best way to express their dissatisfaction with Britain.

On September 6, a committee was appointed "to state the rights of the Colonies . . . and the means most proper to be pursued for obtaining the restoration of them." The committee was made up of two delegates from each colony and included John and Samuel Adams, Roger Sherman, John Jay, Richard Henry Lee, and Edmund Pendleton. On October 14, 1774, the Congress adopted the Declaration of Rights (**document 1**). In its preamble and 10 resolutions, the representatives explained that their resistance to the Intolerable Acts was the result of their concern over the loss of rights. They asserted that the colonists had the right to peaceful assembly and to petition for the redress of grievances. They also opposed keeping a standing army in times of peace.

Following the Declaration of Independence in 1776, many of the states adopted constitutions that included declarations of rights limiting state governments. The Continental Congress was under no such official constraint until 1781 when the Articles of Confederation were adopted. Due to the exigencies of war, Congress quartered Continental soldiers in communities, even though it condemned the practice by the British. Quartering meant that a community provided not only room but also board for troops; the practice represented substantial hardship and expense to the host community because they were paid in depreciated currency. Revolutionary records reveal that food and hospital supplies for the support of the army from October 10, 1775, to May 10, 1776, cost an estimated £200,000. Providence, Rhode Island, was a community so burdened. In a 1779 town meeting, the inhabitants resolved to send a letter (**document 2**) to the Rhode Island delegates to Congress requesting that the United States fund barracks for the American troops. The struggling government was in no position to help the people of Providence; payment for, as well as prohibition of, quartering was contingent upon American victory.

Time: 1 class period

Objectives:

- To introduce original documents and document analysis.

- To examine colonial protests against governmental abuse of power.

Materials Needed:

Documents 1 and 2
Transcription of document 2
Textbook copy of the Constitution and its amendments
Worksheet 1

Procedures:

Some documents are very difficult to read and require close attention. Until the mid-19th century, handwriting and printing were much different in some ways from the way they appear today. The letter "S" creates problems for modern readers since a "long S" or "short S" could be used.

1. Distribute copies of document 1 to the students. Read the document aloud as the students follow. The students should become accustomed to reading a handwritten document by following the teacher's oral reading. When they have completed the reading, ask them to summarize the meaning of each resolution in order. Ask a recorder to list these summaries for the class on the chalkboard.

2. Discuss the following questions with the students.

   a. What are the three sources of the rights of the colonists, according to the authors of this document?

   b. List the rights claimed by the authors of this document.

   c. According to the authors, under the common law, what were the rights of Englishmen?

   d. Is the tone of the document strong or weak? What are your clues to this?

3. Duplicate and distribute document 2 and worksheet 1. Read aloud the transcription in this guide as the students follow their copies of the document.

Exercise 1: The Revolutionary Background of the Bill of Rights

Worksheet 1

Directions: Use a copy of the Constitution and its amendments with document 1 to complete part 1 of the worksheet.

1. Compare and contrast the kinds of rights in the Bill of Rights and document 1.

    a. What rights in the Declaration of Rights are part of the Constitution itself? Refer to the article and section of these rights.

        _____

        _____

    b. What rights in the Declaration of Rights are in the Bill of Rights? Designate which resolution corresponds to which amendment.

        _____

        _____

    c. What rights in the Bill of Rights were omitted from the Declaration of Rights?

        _____

        _____

2. Parliament's Quartering Act was mainly responsible for colonial resistance to quartering troops, but it was standard practice for all armies of the time. Read document 2 to answer the following questions.

    a. What two reasons do the people of Providence give for their request that expenses for quartering troops be borne by the general public?

        _____

        _____

    b. What action, specifically, do the people of Providence request Congress to take before winter approaches?

        _____

        _____

    c. Consider the impact of supporting a military camp in your own household. What impact would having to support several soldiers have on your household? What impact would having soldiers in your house have on your privacy? What other effects would it have?

        _____

        _____

    d. Describe how you might feel toward those households not required to support soldiers.

        _____

        _____

    e. What evidence is there in this document that the quartering of troops by Congress occurred frequently enough and was sufficiently burdensome on citizens that it deserved an amendment to the Constitution? Explain whether you think that an amendment was necessary.

        _____

        _____

Exercise 2
Writing and Adopting the Federal Bill of Rights

Note to the Teacher:

Under the Articles of Confederation, personal liberties were protected by the state constitutions against abuses by state government. As a more powerful, more centralized government emerged at the Constitutional Convention during the summer of 1787, fears grew that state governments would be weakened and personal rights imperiled. As early as June 20, George Mason, author of the Virginia Bill of Rights, raised the issue of federal protection of personal liberties. Charles Pinckney of South Carolina submitted a list of rights to the Committee of Detail on August 20 upon which no action was taken. Pinckney, along with Mason and Elbridge Gerry of Massachusetts, then pressed for piecemeal inclusion of safeguards in the Constitution itself. They succeeded in getting the delegates to adopt clauses guaranteeing trial by jury and writ of habeas corpus and prohibiting bills of attainder, ex post facto laws, and religious tests for federal office.

Unaccountably, it was not until September 12 that Elbridge Gerry proposed and George Mason seconded a motion to include a bill of rights. Weary delegates, eager to get home, voted as state units to unanimously defeat the proposal, believing that state guarantees of rights were adequate protection of civil liberties and that checks and balances in the Constitution would prevent abuses by the federal government.

Believing that a separate statement of rights was necessary, as well as for a variety of other reasons, Mason and Gerry refused to sign the Constitution. Upon his departure from the convention, Mason wrote and published an explanation for his refusal in "Objections to this Constitution of Government," which opened with the criticism, "There is no Declaration of Rights, and the laws of the general government being paramount to the laws and constitution of the several States, the Declaration of Rights in the separate States are no security."

To a populace still embued with revolutionary fervor, a constitution lacking a bill of rights was flawed. Quickly, the Antifederalists took up the demand for addition of a bill of rights as a condition for ratification of the Constitution. Richard Henry Lee asked the Congress of the Confederation to add a bill of rights to the Constitution before forwarding it to the states for ratification; Congress rejected the idea, however, fearful of the confusion this might cause.

Thus the state ratifying conventions became the battlegrounds upon which the fight for a bill of rights was waged. The Federalists believed that a republican government deriving its powers from the people needed no bill, that explicit lists could be used to limit freedoms, and that amendments would be added not simply to extend rights but to fatally weaken the new federal government. Nonetheless, their reasoning did little to relieve Antifederalist anxieties. Although Massachusetts, South Carolina, New Hampshire, Virginia, and New York ratified the Constitution, delegates at those conventions attached amendments along with their instruments of ratification. When North Carolina's constitutional ratifying convention met on August 1, 1788, it decided to defer consideration until Congress added a bill of rights to the Constitution. They appended to their declination a 20-article declaration of rights **(document 3)** as a model for Congress. During the acrimonious debate in Virginia, James Madison yielded to demands and pledged to fight for rights amendments as soon as the Constitution was ratified. With New Hampshire's ratification, the Constitution went into effect. Rather than boycott elections to the new government, Antifederalists ran for office, in part to make certain a bill of rights was passed and to ensure that they would have a share in drafting the amendments with the broadest wording possible.

2

At his inauguration, George Washington asked for amendments to reinforce the rights of free men, confident that Congress would reject dangerous alterations to the federal form of government. After the House convened on April 1, 1789, Representative James Madison honored his commitment by announcing on May 4 his intention to introduce constitutional amendments protecting civil liberties. Although revenue matters took precedence, by June 8, Madison had introduced a plan to enlarge the Constitution to eight articles. He distilled his plan from state bills of rights, the rights recommended by state constitutional ratifying conventions, and historic legal rights. He proposed to incorporate a group of definite guarantees for all the personal liberties that ultimately formed the Bill of Rights in the Constitution without impairing the powers or structure of the federal government. After six weeks of congressional inaction, Madison reintroduced his proposal, which was then referred to a committee composed of one member from each state, including Madison and Roger Sherman of Connecticut. The committee framed the report in one week and presented it to the whole House sitting as the Committee of the Whole. After another delay, the debate began. Sherman preferred to add the rights as amendments to the Constitution, as opposed to Madison's concept of incorporating them. On August 19, the House adopted Sherman's approach. Next, it considered the content of the proposals. Wording of the religion clauses was changed, but the report retained much of Madison's original phrasing. Seventeen amendments were adopted on August 21, 1789, as recorded in the journal of the proceedings of the House (**document 4**).

The Senate received the proposed amendments on August 24 and began to discuss them on September 2. Eliminating Madison's amendment prohibiting states from infringing on personal freedoms and several less significant items, the Senate adopted 12 articles that were returned to the House for concurrence. On September 19, the conference committee, which included Madison and Sherman, swiftly dispensed with the differences between the two versions; the major change was rewording of the religious establishment clause. The conference version was passed by the House on September 24 and by the Senate on the next day. The enrolled original of the House joint resolution proposing 12 amendments (**document 5**) was signed by Speaker of the House Muhlenberg on September 28 and shortly afterwards by John Adams in his role as President of the Senate. This final, fair version is now displayed to the public in the National Archives Rotunda as the Bill of Rights. Copies of this original were forwarded to the states for consideration.

The ratification of the Constitution by Rhode Island and admission of the new state of Vermont raised the number of states needed to ratify the proposed amendments to eleven. On December 15, 1791, Virginia's ratification (**document 6**) provided the two-thirds majority mandated by the Constitution and added to it amendments 3 to 12, now called the Bill of Rights. Personal liberties were protected from violation by Congress and federal officials.

State and local governments, however, were bound only by state bills of rights since Madison's article to extend federal protection to state action had been struck by the Senate. In the case of *Barron v. Baltimore*, 1833, John Marshall reaffirmed that the Fourth Amendment and other federal rights were not binding on the states. As Madison feared, state violations of personal liberties and the tyranny of local majorities had not been resolved by the first 10 amendments. Not until after the adoption of the Fourteenth Amendment would the Bill of Rights be nationalized.

Time: 2 class periods

Objectives:

- To examine the process of writing and approving the Bill of Rights.

- To identify the elements that were eliminated from the contributing drafts.

- To define the strengths of the final document.

Materials Needed:

Documents 3-6
Worksheet 2
A copy of the first 10 amendments to the Constitution

Procedures:

1. Divide the class into groups of three to four students. Distribute a copy of the set of four documents for each group and a copy of worksheet 2 for each student. Direct students to circulate the documents within the group as they complete the worksheet.

2. After the worksheets are completed, review each document with the students.

3. James Madison was concerned that adding a bill of rights to the Constitution as amendments made them more vulnerable than embedding them in the Constitution. Time has proved that, indeed, amendments to the Constitution can be voided, as the Twenty-first Amendment repealed the Eighteenth Amendment. Inclusion of the writ of habeas corpus in the Constitution, however, did not prevent its suspension during the Civil War. Ask students to write a position paper with supporting reasons either approving or opposing Madison's idea to embed change in the Constitution.

4. Direct students to choose for further research from the following topics. They may report their findings orally or in the form of a map or chart when appropriate.

    a. If your state was in the Union at the time, how did it vote on the 12 proposed amendments?

    b. Which of the states in the Union at the time voted for which articles?

    c. Of the states in the Union, which did not ratify any amendments in the 18th century? Why? When did the remaining original states finally ratify?

    d. What is the status of the two amendments that were not ratified at the time?

    e. What amendments, if any, are being suggested for inclusion in the Constitution today?

Exercise 2: Writing and Adopting the Federal Bill of Rights

Worksheet 2

Directions: Use information from documents 3-6 to complete the worksheet.

1. What rights in the first 10 amendments are in:

    a. the North Carolina Declaration of Rights?

        _____

        _____

    b. the 17 amendments approved by the House?

        _____

        _____

    c. the 12 amendments sent to the states?

        _____

        _____

2. Which rights in the North Carolina Declaration did not make it into the first 10 amendments to the Constitution?

    _____

    _____

3. Which rights in the 17 amendments approved by the House did not make it into the first 10 amendments to the Constitution?

    _____

    _____

4. Which rights in the 12 proposed amendments sent to the states did not make it into the first 10 amendments to the Constitution?

    _____

    _____

5. After the adoption of the first 10, list any rights adopted that originally appeared in the:

    a. North Carolina Declaration of Rights

        _____

        _____

    b. 17 amendments adopted by the House

        _____

        _____

    c. 12 amendments ratified by Virginia

        _____

        _____

Exercise 3
The 14th Amendment and Attempts to Nationalize the Bill of Rights

Note to the Teacher:

Following the Civil War, Congress submitted to the states three amendments as part of its Reconstruction program to guarantee equal civil and legal rights to black citizens. On June 16, 1866, the House joint resolution proposing the Fourteen Amendment to the Constitution (**document 7**) was submitted to the states. On July 28, 1868, it was declared ratified and became part of the supreme law of the land.

Congressman John A. Bingham of Ohio, the primary author of the first section of the Fourteenth Amendment, intended that the amendment have a second, broader effect, that of nationalizing the federal Bill of Rights by making it binding upon the states. Jacob Howard of Michigan, who introduced the amendment in the Senate, specifically stated that the privileges and immunities clause would extend to the states "the personal rights guaranteed and secured by the first eight amendments." He was, however, alone in this assertion. Most senators argued that the privileges and immunities clause did not bind the states to the federal Bill of Rights.

Not only did the Fourteenth Amendment fail to extend the Bill of Rights to the states, but it also failed to protect the rights of black citizens. One legacy of Reconstruction was the determined struggle of numerous black and white citizens to make the promise of the Fourteenth Amendment reality. Citizens petitioned and initiated court cases, Congress enacted legislation, and executive branch officers attempted to enforce measures that would guard all citizens' rights. While these citizens would not succeed in empowering the Fourteenth Amendment during Reconstruction, they effectively articulated arguments and offered dissenting opinions that would be the basis for change in the 20th century.

The first case to test the impact of the Fourteenth Amendment on the Bill of Rights began in 1870 when the Butchers Benevolent Association of New Orleans filed a lawsuit against the Crescent City Livestock Landing and Slaughter House Company alleging that the Louisiana legislature had granted to the Crescent City slaughterhouse a monopoly in violation of the Fourteenth Amendment's guarantee of privileges and immunities of U.S. citizenship. The butchers claimed specifically that the state had interfered with "life, liberty, [and] the pursuit of Honorable and just means for promoting happiness and obtaining comfort." The Supreme Court of Louisiana upheld the arguments of the defendant slaughterhouse company and entered judgment in its favor. A petition for a writ of error was allowed by the Supreme Court on May 13, 1870 (**document 8**). On April 14, 1873, in a 5-4 decision, the Court ruled that the Privileges and Immunities Clause of the Fourteenth Amendment was not binding and that protection of ordinary civil liberties was a power reserved to the states. It was not until *Gitlow v. New York* (**document 9**) in 1925 that, through the Due Process Clause of the Fourteenth Amendment, the Bill of Rights would begin to be nationalized.

While the Slaughterhouse cases were moving through the appellate process, the executive branch was attempting to enforce both the Fourteenth and Fifteenth Amendments, protecting civil rights and voting rights. The U.S. Secret Service, part of the Treasury Department, was charged with investigating violations of rights and making recommendations for improvement to the Solicitor's Office of the Department of Justice. **Document 9** is the beginning of a series of four lengthy reports by H. C. Whitley, Chief, Secret Service Division, to Attorney General George Williams. In his report of September 29, 1871, he describes the difficulty of gathering information about the Ku Klux Klan, conveys his

3

agents' reports about oppression of new black citizens by the Klan, and recommends action by the U.S. district attorneys. He expressed his belief that most southerners were law abiding and his expectation that the Klan would die out soon.

Document 10 is the articulate plea of the "colored citizens of Cleveland & vicinity, Tenn.," petitioning Congress to pass legislation to enforce more effectively the Fourteenth Amendment. On January 19, 1874, the petition was referred to the House Committee of the Judiciary where it languished. State legislation had already begun to construct the system of segregation that would be legal until 1954.

Time: 2 class periods

Objectives:

- To identify agents and methods of legal change, including the amendment process, during Reconstruction.

- To examine the limitations of legal change during the era of Reconstruction.

Materials Needed:

Documents 7-10
Worksheet 3
Textbook copy of the U.S. Constitution

Procedures:

1. Ask students to review what their textbooks say about the Civil War amendments and share with them background information on the Fourteenth Amendment from the Note to the Teacher. Ask the class to brainstorm what they consider to be their privileges and immunities as U.S. citizens. List their ideas on the chalkboard.

2. Duplicate a set of the four documents and a worksheet for each student. Direct students to study the documents and the U.S. Constitution and complete the worksheet as a homework assignment.

3. When the students have completed the worksheet, discuss questions they may have. Then, ask the class to consider the four documents as a set and to discuss the following questions:

   a. What privileges and immunities of citizens were of paramount interest to the creators of these documents over 100 years ago? How are they similar or different from the list brainstormed by the class?

   b. Ours is a nation of laws that people may disagree with and work to change but may not disobey with impunity. What do these documents reveal about the legal avenues available to people of the Reconstruction era for pursuing an extension of the privileges and immunities of citizens? What do these documents reveal about the methods of those who opposed the extension of such privileges?

   c. It is sometimes said that we stand on the shoulders of those who have gone before us. Citizens of the Reconstruction era failed in their efforts to extend Bill of Rights protections against state acts. Were their efforts futile or did later personal liberties advocates or civil rights movements benefit from the efforts of these earlier citizens?

4. Extended activities:

   a. Assign one or two students to find out what political parties have said about citizens' rights in their party platforms in a particular election and report their findings to the class. For example, they may wish to locate the black civil rights planks of the 1872 Republican and Democratic platforms alluded to in the Cleveland, TN, petition. Major library systems and university libraries should have the two-volume *National Party Platforms: 1840-1984* and may have recent Republican Party official convention proceedings. Democratic state committees have the party's most recent platforms. For another source, students may wish to contact the Democratic National Committee's research office or the Republican National Committee's archives office in Washington, DC, or visit their Web sites.

   b. Assign a student to check the current constitution of your state to see what rights are guaranteed to citizens of the state and to share the information with the class. In the report, the student should compare and contrast state privileges and immunities with those of U.S. citizens and compare and contrast the protection provided in the state bill of rights with the liberties brainstormed by the class in procedure 1.

Exercise 3: The 14th Amendment and Attempts to Nationalize the Bill of Rights

Worksheet 3

Directions: Use information from documents 7-10 and Article V of the U.S. Constitution to complete the worksheet.

Document 7: The Fourteenth Amendment

1. What branch of the government initiates a constitutional amendment?

   _____

2. How much of a majority is required in each house of Congress for the proposed amendment to advance?

   _____

3. How much of a majority in the state legislatures is required for ratification of an amendment?

   _____

4. According to section 1, you are a citizen of what two jurisdictions?

   _____

5. What branch of the government is responsible for enabling a ratified amendment to be enforced, according to section 5?

   _____

Document 8: Writ of Error

1. In your own words, explain what right the petitioner claimed under the Fourteenth Amendment.

   _____

   _____

2. In your own words, explain what the legislature of Louisiana did that violated the petitioner's rights.

   _____

   _____

3. What did the petitioners ask of the Supreme Court?

   _____

   _____

Document 9: Secret Service Report

1. According to the report, what steps is the government taking to protect the rights of new black citizens?

    _____

    _____

2. What is the authorization that legally permitted the Secret Service agents to infiltrate the Ku Klux Klan?

    _____

    _____

3. What actions of the Klan are the Secret Service agents investigating?

    _____

    _____

4. Why is it so difficult for the Secret Service agents to infiltrate the Klan?

    _____

    _____

5. According to the report, why is the Klan so effective, and why haven't law-abiding citizens challenged the Klan?

    _____

    _____

6. What steps do you think the Attorney General could take, based on the information in this report?

    _____

    _____

Document 10: Petition

1. What means did the citizens of Cleveland, TN, use to try to improve their living conditions?

    _____

    _____

2. What types of state laws abridged Tennessee black citizens' rights in 1874?

    _____

    _____

3

3. According to the petition, how were such laws hurting white citizens as well?

_____

_____

4. What evidence do the petitioners offer to substantiate their claim that black Union veterans have fewer rights than white Confederate veterans?

_____

_____

5. Why do you believe the petitioners mentioned the 1872 party platforms and election?

_____

_____

6. What other methods to push enforcement of the Fourteenth Amendment were available to these citizens at this time?

_____

_____

7. Underline the adjectives in the petition.

   a. What pattern emerges?

   _____

   _____

   b. What is the tone assumed toward the federal government? the state government?

   _____

   _____

   c. What words, in the main body of the petition, were underlined by the writers? Why do you think they underlined them?

   _____

   _____

   d. List emotionally charged words or expressions that the petitioners use to try to persuade the Congress to pass enforcing legislation.

   _____

   _____

Exercise 4
The First Amendment

Note to the Teacher:

Our most personal liberties – freedom of religion, freedom of expression, freedom of the press, the right to peaceful assembly, and the right to petition the government – are protected by the First Amendment. The first ratified addition to the Constitution and the first of the amendments to be made binding upon the states by the due process clause of the Fourteenth Amendment, the First Amendment enjoys a primacy belonging to no other. Indeed, Justice Wiley Rutledge in *Thomas v. Collins* conferred the First Amendment with a "preferred position" in the hierarchy of rights. Yet, as favored as the First Amendment is, and as absolute as the language of the amendment is, there are limits to the freedoms guaranteed therein. The rights of the individual are balanced against the common good as conflicts arise.

Freedom of religion is the first right guaranteed in the First Amendment. The first clause prohibits the establishment of religion. In 1947 the Board of Education of Ewing Township, NJ, resolved to pay for the busing of all high school students whether they attended public or parochial school since there was no high school in the district. Arch Everson challenged the resolution all the way to the Supreme Court, charging that public monies were being used to support church-run schools. The American Civil Liberties Union was one of several groups that filed an amicus curiae brief supporting Everson's suit **(document 11)**. In a 5-4 decision upholding Ewing Township, the Court ruled, in the words of Justice Hugo Black, that "The First Amendment has erected a wall between church and state. That wall must be kept high and impregnable. We could not approve the slightest breach. New Jersey has not breached it here."

The second religion clause guarantees free exercise of religion, yet it, like other personal rights, has not been uniformly sustained. In times of war, there often is conflict between national interest and individual conscience. During the early part of the Civil War, when Union forces were rarely successful, Ulysses S. Grant seemed to be a winning general. Oftentimes, he resorted to expedient measures to ensure victory. To curtail peddlers who were trading with the Confederacy for black market cotton, Grant issued on December 17, 1862, the ill-worded General Order No. 11. The order expelled all Jews from the Department of the Tennessee. Within the day, officers of his command were asking if the order banished Jewish sutlers (contract suppliers), enlisted men, officers, and "the governor of one of the western states." It prompted Philip Trounstine, a Jewish captain in the 5th Ohio Cavalry, to resign his commission, writing,

> I cannot help feeling that as I owe filial affection to my parents, Devotion to my Religion, and a deep regard for the opinion of my friends and feeling that I can no longer bear the Taunts and malice of those to whom my religious opinions are known, brought on by the effect that order has instilled into their minds.

In the most serious reaction to the order, 30 Jewish men and their families were expelled from their homes in Paducah, KY. As telegrams and letters arrived in Washington protesting the order, Lincoln ordered Grant's commanding officer, Major General Henry W. Halleck, to revoke the order, which he did in a telegram on January 4, 1863. Resolutions condemning the order were introduced by Representative George H. Pendleton of Ohio in the House and Senator Lazarus W. Powell of Kentucky in the Senate **(document 12)**. They were tabled since the countermanding order was being circulated.

During the Second World War, patriotism was such an important issue that free exercise was again questioned. The Board of Education of West Virginia adopted a resolution on January 2, 1942, requiring

4

all students to salute the flag or face expulsion. Children who were Jehovah's Witnesses resisted on the grounds that it was an act of idolatry in violation of their religious belief. In 1940 the Supreme Court had sustained a Pennsylvania flag salute law in *Minersville v. Gobitis*, but in 1943 the Court reversed its opinion in *West Virginia v. Barnette*. Justice Robert Jackson wrote the majority opinion, saying,

> We think the action of the local authorities in compelling the flag salute and pledge transcends constitutional limitations on their power and invades the sphere of intellect and spirit which it is the purpose of the First Amendment to our Constitution to reserve from all official control.

Document 13 is the court mandate ordering West Virginia to readmit the children to school.

In practice, the freedoms of speech and press have never been absolute. In an often quoted passage from Justice Oliver Wendell Holmes' decision in *Schenck v. United States* (1919), he wrote,

> The most stringent protection of free speech would not protect a man in falsely shouting fire in a theatre and causing a panic . . . the question in every case is whether the words used are used in such circumstances and are of such a nature as to create a clear and present danger that they will bring about the substantive evils that Congress has a right to prevent.

In times of national emergency, the threshold for "clear and present danger" has been lowered, and seditious language defined more broadly. For example, during the presidency of John Adams, when war with France appeared imminent, the Congress passed the Alien and Sedition Acts curbing free speech and free press. Ten convictions followed including that of Thomas Cooper, who was indicted in April 1800, found guilty of printing comments about the President that were seditious libel under the law, and sentenced to six months in prison and a $400 fine. The laws were criticized in the Virginia and Kentucky Resolutions and by the Republican-Democrat Party led by Thomas Jefferson. When he was elected president, Jefferson allowed the Acts to expire without reviving them. In 1825 Cooper petitioned Congress for restoration of his fine with interest. A Select committee reported on his case to the House with the recommendation (**document 14**) that his petition be granted, and it was.

Again during World War I, espionage and sedition acts were adopted that resulted in nearly 1,000 convictions. **Document 15**, the Espionage Act of June 15, 1917, defined espionage and, in section 12, denied the use of the mails to newspapers, periodicals, and other materials that were unpatriotic, critical, or treasonous. Many publications were scrutinized, including an article about government energy use published on November 12, 1917, in the *Los Angeles Daily Times* (**document 16**). Justice Department officials investigated *The Finished Mystery*, a pacifist book published by the Jehovah's Witnesses (**document 17**), and warned bookstores and newsstands in Atlanta against carrying it. The postmistress of Melbourne, FL, sent a poster (**document 18**) and two issues of *The Favorite Magazine* along with a letter asking the Postmaster General, "Are the inclosed [sic] periodicals in accordance with postal rules and regulations?" Through six cases, including *Schenck*, the Supreme Court sustained the federal acts, decisions that have yet to be overruled.

States also had laws restraining free speech, particularly treasonable speech. In July 1919, in the midst of the Red Scare, Benjamin Gitlow was indicted under the New York criminal anarchy statute for distributing Marxist literature. In *Gitlow v. New York*, the Supreme Court sustained his conviction. In writing the opinion, the Court unexpectedly opened up the application of the Bill of Rights to the states saying,

> For present purposes we may and do assume that freedom of speech and of the press — which are protected by the First Amendment from abridgment by Congress — are among the fundamental personal rights and "liberties" protected by the due process clause of the Fourteenth Amendment from impairment by the States.

Document 19 is an inquiry to the Clerk of the Supreme Court from an Ohio judge about the decision.

In more recent years, the Vietnam conflict put a strain on the right to free expression. Public school students John and Mary Beth Tinker of Des Moines, IA, belonged to a family that actively opposed the war in Vietnam. To demonstrate grief at the mounting casualties and to express support for a Christmas truce, they wore 2-inch-wide black armbands to school on December 17, 1965. They were suspended by their principal, who was implementing a ruling adopted by the Des Moines School Board that forbade the wearing of armbands to school. The case was appealed to the Supreme Court accompanied by the transcript of John Tinker's testimony in the lower court (**document 20**). In 1969 the court ruled that the school board had improperly abridged John and Mary Beth Tinker's right to symbolic expression under the First Amendment.

Justice Hugo Black observed in *Bridges v. California* that "It is the prized American privilege to speak one's mind, although not always with perfect good taste, on all public institutions." Comedians Tom and Dick Smothers encountered no governmental restraint on their satirical commentaries directed against the war. Indeed, the network censors of CBS gave them more difficulty than did the administration. Nonetheless, they confessed in a letter to President Lyndon Johnson (**document 21**) that they had overstepped the bounds of propriety, shielded by the First Amendment.

Time: 2 class periods

Objectives:

- To identify and analyze the religion, expression, and petition clauses of the First Amendment.

- To develop and apply vocabulary related to First Amendment issues.

- To extract information from a poster and a petition.

Materials Needed:

Documents 11-21 and 36
Worksheet 4
Written Document Analysis worksheet
Poster Analysis worksheet

Procedures:

1. Duplicate and distribute worksheet 4 for students to complete.
   Worksheet 4 Key: 1. preferred position, 2. absolutism, 3. clear and present danger, 4. wall of separation, 5. prior restraint, 6. balancing, 7. establishment of religion, 8. peaceful assembly, 9. bad tendency, 10. freedom of speech, 11. freedom of the press, 12. symbolic speech, 13. free exercise of religion, 14. petition for redress of grievances, 15. First Amendment

2. Make a listing of the headings of documents 11-21 and place centrally on the classroom bulletin board. This procedure need not be completed all at once, but it is intended that each student will have the opportunity to review many if not all of the documents.

   a. You may wish to create a worksheet listing the document number for documents 11-21, which will look like the listing on the bulletin board. Duplicate a classroom set of documents 11-21. (This activity can be modified to use any combination of these documents.) Either on one day or several days, rotate the documents so that each student examines all of the documents and decides which of the First Amendment freedoms are illustrated in each document. As the class studies a document and shares information found in the document, they should complete the bulletin board chart.

b. Excluding document 18, instruct students to choose any two documents and to complete a Written Document Analysis worksheet for each.

c. Ask the students to answer the following questions on a separate sheet of paper and attach it to the worksheets for the two documents they have selected.

- What do you feel the mood of the country was toward the problem or topic addressed in this document?

- Has that mood changed today? Explain your answer. (Document 21 is an excellent example for this activity.)

d. Place a copy of the document and one of the students' two analysis worksheets on the bulletin board beside each document heading to complete the display.

3. Duplicate and distribute to students the Poster Analysis worksheet. Post document 18 and ask students to complete the worksheet based on the information in that poster.

4. Documents 10, 14, and 36 contain petitions to Congress. Ask students to study the documents and then to discuss the following questions.

a. What rules of form do these petitions appear to follow?

b. What similarities in form or content exist between these petitions? How do you account for these similarities?

c. What differences in form or content are there among these petitions? How do you account for these differences?

Exercise 4: The First Amendment

Worksheet 4

Directions: Use information from documents 11-21, your textbook's section on the First Amendment, and the following phrases to fill the blanks of the worksheet.

absolutism

bad tendency

balancing

clear and present danger

establishment of religion

First Amendment

free exercise of religion

freedom of speech

freedom of the press

peaceful assembly

petition for redress of grievances

preferred position

prior restraint

symbolic speech

wall of separation

1. An interpretation that explains the relation of the First Amendment rights to other rights when they conflict.

    _____

2. An interpretation that says Congress may never restrict First Amendment rights in any way.

    _____

3. The interpretation that says that free speech may not be limited unless there is obvious immediate danger to society.

    _____

4. The interpretation that the church and state never mix.

    _____

5. Requirement that the press receive approval before material is published.

    _____

6. The interpretation that weighs individual rights against the good of society.

    _____

7. The first of the religion clauses of the First Amendment.

    _____

4

8. First Amendment right that guarantees nonviolent demonstrations.

_____

9. Speech that may cause acts in violation of the law.

_____

10. First Amendment right that allows citizens to criticize the government.

_____

11. First Amendment right that protects newspapers and the media.

_____

12. Nonverbal, unpublished expression, such as John Tinker's black armband, that is protected by the First Amendment.

_____

13. The second of the religion clauses of the First Amendment.

_____

14. Right to request in writing that the government correct a problem.

_____

15. The common theme of questions 1-14.

_____

Exercise 5
The Second Amendment

Note to the Teacher:

The right to keep and bear arms has been a hotly debated topic in recent years, so it is useful to examine what the government has said in its own words and the actions it has taken.

In the years preceding the Revolutionary War, two approaches to colonial defense came into conflict. English tradition traces the use of the militia as a measure of providing for the common defense as far back as King Alfred in the ninth century. The practice was introduced into the English colonies at the time of the first settlement, obliging adult male inhabitants to possess arms and ammunition and to meet to drill at appointed times. Great Britain also relied on a standing army, even during rare times of peace, to maintain its growing, far-flung colonial possessions.

Revolutionary critics of British practice believed that professional soldiers were a threat to liberty and that militiamen constituted an adequate security force. When the Crown sent British troops to Boston to enforce the Intolerable Acts, the Continental Congress denounced the action in Resolution Nine of the Declaration of Rights (**document 1**), asserting that "the keeping of a Standing army in these colonies, in times of peace, without the consent of the legislature of that colony, in which such army is kept is against the law." Jefferson echoed the grievance in the Declaration of Independence, charging of King George III that "He has kept among us, in times of peace, standing armies without the consent of our legislatures."

With independence, the new states drafted constitutions that included provisions regarding the organization and control of state militias. In most cases, the right to keep and bear arms was related to military duty, a provision for the common defense. Nonetheless, there was a strong current of sentiment that a citizen had the individual right to arm himself for his own defense. During the debate over the 1780 Massachusetts Declaration of Right, the wording of the arms clause provoked many towns to petition for more precise language that would make the keeping and bearing of arms a personal right.

In Article I, section 8, clauses 15 and 16, the Constitution endows Congress with the power to federalize state militias and to organize, arm, and discipline them when federalized. Antifederalists and state governments were concerned that the federal government might abuse this power and pushed for guarantees of the right of militias to arm. Although the bulk of the amendments Madison proposed were general safeguards of individual rights, the use in the Second Amendment of the collective phrase, "right of the people," hints that Madison viewed this as a right of militiamen more than a general guarantee to all citizens.

Over the years since its adoption, the Supreme Court has consistently interpreted the Second Amendment as a state's right rather than an individual's. For example, in *United States v. Miller* (1939), a case that challenged the legality of the National Firearms Act, Justice James McReynolds wrote that, in the absence of evidence that possession of a sawed-off, double barreled 12-gauge shotgun had "some reasonable relationship to the preservation or efficiency of a well regulated militia, we cannot say that the Second Amendment guarantees the right to keep and bear such an instrument. Certainly it is not within judicial notice that this weapon is part of the ordinary military equipment or that its use could contribute to the common defense."

Accordingly, the states and Congress are unrestricted, outside of the province of the militia, in their power to regulate citizens' rights to own and bear arms. Yet Congress has rarely attempted to regulate weapons. The National Firearms Act of 1934 prohibited the use or possession of gangster-type weapons. Later on, the Federal Firearms Act regulated interstate sales of common firearms. In November 1963, following Lee Harvey Oswald's assassination of President John F. Kennedy with a mail-order rifle, there

5

was immediate demand by an outraged public to enact more stringent controls on such weapons. **Document 22** is a letter from Acting General Counsel Lawrence Jones of the Department of Commerce, whose Bureau of Alcohol, Tobacco and Firearms was responsible for enforcing the Federal Firearms Act, to Senator Warren G. Magnuson, Chairman of the Committee of Commerce, which was considering two bills to amend the Federal Firearms Act.

Time: 1 class period

Objectives:

- To identify and examine issues related to the Second Amendment.
- To study federal decision-making techniques.

Materials Needed:

Document 22

Procedures:

1. Share with students the background information from the Note to the Teacher and ask students to review what their textbooks say about the Second Amendment. Since the Second Amendment is historically linked to the issue of states rights, review with students your state's firearms laws.

2. Duplicate and distribute copies of document 22 to each student. Discuss the following questions with the class.

   a. What changes in the Federal Firearms Act does S. 2345 propose?

   b. What changes in the Federal Firearms Act does amendment #335 to S. 1975 propose?

   c. What changes to S. 2345 does Mr. Jones suggest?

   d. What problems does Mr. Jones foresee with S. 2345?

   e. According to Mr. Jones, what are the advantages of amendment #335 to S. 1975?

   f. What reasons do you think Senator Magnuson had for requesting comments of Mr. Jones?

   g. Why do you think two bills were introduced on the same issue rather than just one?

3. Assign students a written exercise giving the following directions: Imagine you are Senator Magnuson. You have decided which amendment you will endorse and hope to convince fellow members of the Committee on Commerce to support your choice. Write a statement explaining which amendment you are backing, giving reasons for your choice and objections you have to the other amendment.

4. Discuss with your students whether, to protect public safety, the common good takes precedence over individual rights. What are the proper limits on public good and on individual exercise of rights? Is this a resolvable question? Literature expounding the arguments both for and against gun control is available from various organizations. Ask for volunteers to trace the interpretation of the Second Amendment, including the following cases, and to report their findings to the class.

   a. *United States v. Cruikshank*, 92 U.S. 542 (1875)

   b. *Presser v. Illinois* 116 U.S. 252 (1886)

   c. *United States v. Miller*, 307 U.S. 174 (1939)

Exercise 6
Due Process and the Rights of the Accused

Note to the Teacher:

There is little about the petitioner or the crime for which he stands charged that commends itself. But the cause of due process is ill-served when a disturbed, little-educated indigent is sentenced to lengthy prison terms largely on the basis of a confession which he gave without being first advised of his right to counsel. This petition, therefore, squarely raises the question of whether the right to counsel turns upon request; whether, in other words, the knowledgeable suspect will be given constitutional preference over those members of society most in need of assistance.

This observation was made by the lawyer for the accused in the petition for a writ of certiorari in the case of Ernesto A. Miranda, but it would have been almost as appropriate in the cases of Clarence Earl Gideon or William Henry Furman. Over the past decades, from the Scottsboro cases through the present, the Bill of Rights has gradually been extended to protect criminal defendants from unlawful state action.

In 1932, in the first of the Scottsboro appeals to come before the Supreme Court, *Powell v. Alabama*, the Court ruled that the right to counsel in a capital case was fundamental to due process. The indigent defendants were not provided adequate time to hire lawyers, and the court-requested lawyers had inadequate time to prepare a defense. It appeared that the decision incorporated the Sixth Amendment into the Constitution through the Fourteenth Amendment, but, 10 years later, the Supreme Court rejected incorporation of the right to counsel in *Betts v. Brady*.

In the early 1960s, the Supreme Court began to incorporate the Fifth and Sixth Amendments into the Constitution. *Malloy v. Hogan* extended the right against self-incrimination to the states in 1964. The Sixth Amendment was incorporated in the landmark case of *Gideon v. Wainright*.

Clarence Earl Gideon, an indigent with five prior convictions, was arrested for breaking and entering a pool hall in Bay Harbor, FL, in June 1961. At the beginning of his trial in August, Gideon requested that the judge appoint a lawyer to defend him, but the judge refused, since Florida law provided for free lawyers only in capital cases. Gideon unsuccessfully defended himself, was convicted, and was sent to the Florida state prison. Although Gideon only had an eighth grade education, he filed a petition for a writ of habeas corpus, which was denied by Florida. He then petitioned the Supreme Court for a writ of certiorari but failed to use the required form; his request was returned with a Supreme Court style manual. Writing on prison stationery and following the samples in the booklet, Gideon resubmitted his request in January 1962. When the lawyers for the state of Florida replied, he rejoined on April 19, 1962, in **document 23**. Gideon requested a review in forma pauperis, and the Supreme Court appointed Abe Fortas to represent Gideon. Fortas' arguments convinced the Court to reverse *Betts* and in a unanimous decision required states to provide counsel for indigent felony defendants. Gideon was retried in Bay Harbor, his case presented by a lawyer, and he was found innocent, as he had steadfastly claimed all along.

Gideon v. Wainright did not answer all questions about the right to counsel, significantly, at which stage in the trial the right began. *Escobedo v. Illinois* extended the right to counsel to the time at which a suspect was questioned by police. *Escobedo* was refined and superseded, however, by the historic case of *Miranda v. Arizona*. Ernesto Miranda, a mentally retarded indigent, was accused by police in March 1963 of kidnapping and rape. Prevented from talking with a lawyer prior to questioning, he made a confession without realizing he had the right to remain silent. The case came to the Supreme Court on a writ of certiorari (a Supreme Court order requesting a lower court to send their records of a case).

6

As in Gideon's case, Miranda applied for review in forma pauperis, swearing in an affidavit (**document 24**) that he required assistance because of his poverty. In a 5-4 decision that has been sustained consistently since Chief Justice Earl Warren rendered the decision on June 13, 1966, the Court ruled in favor of Miranda. The decision extended the Sixth Amendment right to counsel to a suspect from the moment of arrest and questioning, and it obliged the police to advise suspects of their rights to guarantee their privilege against self-incrimination.

The Eighth Amendment prohibits cruel and unusual punishment and has been incorporated in part to prevent capricious or arbitrary imposition of the death penalty. Capital punishment itself is not regarded as cruel and unusual. But the landmark case of *Furman v. Georgia* in 1972 led to a 5-year moratorium on the death penalty, when the Supreme Court struck down the states' capital punishment laws of all cases then before the Court, saying they gave too much latitude to juries and judges in sentencing. Subsequently, the states revised their laws to conform with the Furman decision and resumed imposing and executing death sentences. When Furman appealed his case to the Supreme Court, a comprehensive transcript of his Chatham County, GA, trial record was forwarded, including the grand jury's indictment, the trial jury's verdict, and the judge's death sentence (**document 25**). The Furman case also forced the federal government to reevaluate capital federal offenses. In 1983, Senator Strom Thurmond introduced S. 1765, a bill establishing constitutional procedures for imposing capital punishment. **Document 26** is the Legislative Notice for S. 1765, a summation of the proposed bill and the issues it raises, which was published prior to the vote in the Senate. The bill passed the Senate 63-32 but failed to pass the House.

Time: 2 to 3 class periods

Objectives:

- To master legal vocabulary.

- To trace the evolution of the incorporation of the Fifth and Sixth Amendments through the Fourteenth Amendment.

- To collect and interpret statistical information.

- To write an interior monologue.

Materials Needed:

Documents 23-26
Worksheet 5
Worksheet 6
Written Document Analysis worksheet, p. 13
Textbook copy of the U.S. Constitution

Procedures:

1. Introduce the lesson by defining the expression "due process." Ask students to locate and identify in the U.S. Constitution the amendments that define due process and equal protection.

2. Many terms in these documents and in the background reading of the cases need to be identified before students can read about Gideon, Miranda, and Furman. Duplicate and

distribute Worksheet 5 and assign students to define the terms listed. After they have completed the worksheet, divide the class into groups of four. Divide the terms into lists of 14 words and give each student group a list to construct into a crossword puzzle. Make copies of all the puzzles for all of the students. After the students have mastered the legal vocabulary, you may wish to invite a lawyer or judge of the state supreme court to speak to your class about one or two due process cases originating in your home state. Alternately, you may wish to contact your local bar association to enter some of your students into mock trial competition.

3. Divide the class into groups containing two or three students. Duplicate documents 23-26 and four copies of the Written Document Analysis worksheet for each group. Instruct each group to analyze all of the documents.

4. Distribute worksheet 6 to all students. Ask them to complete as much as possible of the worksheet with information found in the documents. For homework, assign them to review their textbooks or to go to the library or online and research for the remaining information. Discuss the worksheet in class, clarifying any points on which there is confusion.

5. After reviewing the Furman case, ask students to role-play one of the following figures in the case and to write an interior monologue about their reasoning and emotions as they make decisions about the life of William Henry Furman:

    a. Walter A. Fulmer, foreman of the grand jury, on indicting Furman for murder

    b. Thomas V. Dye, foreman of the trial jury, on convicting Furman of murder

    c. Judge Dunbar Harrison, trial judge, on sentencing Furman to death by electrocution

6. The force of the *Miranda* decision has withstood the test of time, although some of the particulars have been modified to balance the needs of law enforcement officers with the rights of the accused. To highlight the differences in police procedures since *Miranda*, show an old gangster movie or a television program set before *Miranda*. Then assign the students to write an essay defining where the needs of society would be more compelling than the rights of the accused.

7. Extended activity: Ask for several student volunteers to collect the following statistical information, to place it on maps or graphs, and to interpret their findings to the class. Amnesty International, the American Civil Liberties Union, the Southern Poverty Law Center, and the NAACP Legal Defense and Education Fund are good sources for this information.

    a. Which states do not have the death penalty?

    b. Which states have the death penalty, but have never imposed the death sentence?

    c. Which states have the death penalty and have convicts waiting on death row for execution, but have not executed anyone since 1977?

    d. Which states have the death penalty and have executed convicts since 1977?

    e. How many prisoners are on death row in each state?

    f. What is the method of execution for each state?

    g. Of the total number of executions since 1977, how many were voluntary?

    h. For each of the persons executed, what was his or her race, and what was the race of his or her victim?

6

Exercise 6: Due Process and the Rights of the Accused

Worksheet 5

Directions: Refer to your textbook and a dictionary and define the following legal terms:

affidavit _____

affirm _____

amicus curiae _____

appeal _____

appellant _____

appellee _____

capital punishment _____

case law _____

charge _____

circuit court _____

civil law _____

common law _____

complaint _____

concurring opinion _____

conviction _____

counsel (n.) _____

criminal law _____

cross-examination _____

defendant _____

deposition _____

dissenting opinion _____

federal crime _____

felony _____

grand jury _____

indictment _____

in forma pauperis _____

interrogation _____

jurisdiction _____

jury _____

larceny _____

libel _____

litigants _____

majority opinion _____

misdemeanor _____

perjury _____

petitioner _____

plaintiff _____

plea _____

precedent _____

prosecute _____

public defender _____

remand _____

respondent _____

reverse _____

sentence _____

slander _____

stare decisis _____

statute _____

superior court _____

testimony _____

trial docket _____

verdict _____

warrant _____

witness _____

writ _____

writ of certiorari _____

writ of habeas corpus _____

Exercise 6: Due Process and the Rights of the Accused

Worksheet 6

Directions: Use the documents, your textbook, and library reference tools to collect the following data.

	Gideon	Miranda	Furman
Facts			
What crime is he accused of committing?			
When and where does the crime occur?			
Issues			
What right does the accused believe he had been denied?			
Is there a basis for the Supreme Court to review this case?			
What Bill of Rights issue does the Court have to decide?			
Arguments			
What arguments do the accused offer?			
What arguments do the states offer?			
Decision			
What is the Court's decision?			
What reasons does the Court give for its decision?			
What is the effect of the decision on the accused?			
What is the effect of the decision on law enforcement?			
What is the effect of the decision on criminal justice systems?			
What is the effect of the decision on the power of the states?			

Exercise 7
Rights of Minors

Note to the Teacher:

The Ninth Amendment guarantees that rights not enumerated in the Constitution are retained by the people. To identify these rights and give them legal status, statutes have been adopted, amendments added, Presidential proclamations issued, and court opinions written. Rights of citizens under the age of 18 have been secured in this piecemeal manner.

During the 20th century, the federal government has grappled with defining what a right is and what rights minors may have. The first issue that prompted government action was child labor. By 1910, children between the ages of 10 and 15 made up 18.4 percent of the total labor force of the United States, according to census information. The National Child Labor Committee (NCLC), organized in New York City in 1904, investigated child labor conditions and lobbied for the end of child labor. Additional support was provided by muckrakers who publicized the deplorable working conditions in books such as John Spargo's *The Bitter Cry of the Children*, published in 1906. In 1908, photographer Lewis W. Hine was hired by the NCLC to visually document children's working conditions. Over the opposition of business, supporters of states' rights, and President Wilson, the NCLC convinced Congress to establish the Children's Bureau in 1912 and to pass the Keating-Owen Federal Child Labor Law in 1916. Although Congress approved a joint resolution proposing a child labor amendment to the Constitution (**document 27**), it was never ratified by the necessary three-quarters of the state legislatures.

The broader issue of health emerged later in the century. Research and development of medicines was largely conducted by private foundations during times of peace. The federal government's first significant action was in 1955 when Congress passed the Poliomyelitis Vaccination Act, which allocated $30 million to the Public Health Service to distribute to the states for the purchase of polio vaccine to be administered to children and adults. President Dwight D. Eisenhower was reluctant to approve the measure because he feared it would lead to socialized medicine. He believed that the more appropriate federal role was to draw public attention to children's health. A Child Health Day proclamation of 1956 was intended to encourage American awareness of children's health issues and to salute the international contribution to children's health care of UNICEF (**document 28**).

Since the end of World War II, the federal government's role in education has expanded, in part to guarantee for all American students the right to the best education available, in part to ensure the security of the nation. On October 4, 1957, the Soviet Union placed the artificial satellite *Sputnik I* into Earth orbit. The U.S. public was astonished by the Soviet achievement and feared that the national defense had been compromised by inadequate science education in the public schools. As a result, Congress passed the National Defense Education Act, which President Eisenhower signed on September 2, 1958 (**document 29**).

The legal rights of minors emerged in a series of Supreme Court interpretations. Beginning in 1899, juvenile courts were established as a reform measure to separate youthful offenders from older lawbreakers. The juvenile justice system balances justice with the doctrine of parens patriae, under which the court is supposed to act as a parent protecting the interests of the juvenile. In the case of 15-year-old Gerald Gault, the juvenile court judge sentenced him to state reform school until he reached the age of majority, a 6-year sentence, for an obscene phone call (**document 30**). Gault's case was appealed to the Supreme Court, which reversed the lower courts' decisions. Justice Abe Fortas wrote the opinion that found the juvenile court had deprived Gault of due process in denying him basic legal rights including notice of the charges, right to counsel, right to confrontation and cross-examination, privilege against self-incrimination, the right to a transcript of the proceedings, and the right to appellate review.

7

School systems, too, are required to accord students a minimum amount of due process as a result of *Goss v. Lopez*, 1975. The Supreme Court, in a 5-4 decision, ruled that students have a right to an education. The state of Ohio was obliged to provide students with a hearing before suspending them from school for misconduct for up to 10 days. A broader range of rights may be granted to students by local school boards or state law, but not narrower. **Document 31** is a letter written to the Supreme Court prior to the decision in *Goss. v. Lopez*. The Clerk of the Supreme Court responded by referring Ralph Evans to the attorneys in the case for their legal briefs since the Court had no copies.

Time: 1 to 2 class periods

Objectives:

- To discuss rights and liberties not enumerated in the Bill of Rights.

- To examine processes by which non-enumerated rights are recognized.

- To distinguish rights of minors from rights of adults under the Constitution.

Materials Needed:

Documents 27-31
Written Document Analysis worksheet, p. 13

Procedures:

1. Divide the class into five groups and instruct each group to examine one of the documents from this exercise. Each group should complete the Written Document Analysis worksheet, then answer the following questions.

    a. What right (or rights) of minors has been described in this document?

    b. What group or individual is advancing the rights of minors in this document?

    c. What legal avenues are being pursued to ensure rights of minors, according to this document?

2. Ask each group to share its findings with the class, then, as a whole class, brainstorm a list of rights (enumerated and not enumerated) that have been accorded to minors in the United States. List these on the chalkboard.

3. Arrange for a lawyer or juvenile court spokesperson to address the class about the reasoning behind the juvenile justice system, differences between juvenile and regular courts, and due process procedures followed by your local jurisdiction to protect minors.

4. Extended activities: Ask students to select one of the following activities for further research and to share their findings in an oral report.

    a. If your local school board or state department of education has a written list of students' rights and responsibilities, try to discover how they were developed, when they were adopted, and what topics are covered. Are rights other than the due process ones mandated by *Goss v. Lopez* addressed in the listing, for instance rights of learners in instructional matters? Are the topics of the students rights and responsibilities still timely, or are revisions needed?

b. If the school does not have such a list, find out whether the student government has a student rights committee and why no such document has been compiled. Students may wish to work through the student government association with the faculty advisor and administration to adopt a statement of students' rights and responsibilities, and to inform the student body through the school newspaper or perhaps through a special assembly.

c. Contact the school librarian or counseling office about the possibility of preparing and displaying a small exhibit that illustrates the theme of "The Constitution and Students' Rights."

d. Compare and contrast the methods used by children's advocates and black citizens to extend rights under the Fourteenth Amendment.

5. Instituted as a reform more than a 100 years ago, the juvenile justice system has been criticized frequently in recent years. Among the grounds for criticism are the continued lack of full adult constitutional guarantees for juvenile defendants, the absence of rules to deal with heinous juvenile crime, and the problem of defining the age of juveniles. Identify the arguments for and against maintaining the juvenile courts in their present form. Many national periodicals have current articles on the subject. You may also check the Department of Justice Web site at **www.usdoj.gov** and search on "juvenile justice."

H. J. Res. 184

Sixty-eighth Congress of the United States of America;

At the First Session,

Begun and held at the City of Washington on Monday, the third day of December, one thousand nine hundred and twenty-three.

JOINT RESOLUTION
Proposing an amendment to the Constitution of the United States.

Resolved by the Senate and House of Representatives of the United States of America in Congress assembled (two-thirds of each House concurring therein), That the following article is proposed as an amendment to the Constitution of the United States, which, when ratified by the legislatures of three-fourths of the several States, shall be valid to all intents and purposes as a part of the Constitution:

"ARTICLE —

"SECTION 1. The Congress shall have power to limit, regulate, and prohibit the labor of persons under eighteen years of age.

"SEC. 2. The power of the several States is unimpaired by this article except that the operation of State laws shall be suspended to the extent necessary to give effect to legislation enacted by the Congress."

F H GILLETT
Speaker of the House of Representatives.

ALBERT B. CUMMINS
President pro tempore of the Senate.

I certify that this Joint Resolution originated in the House of Representatives.

WM TYLER PAGE
Clerk.

Exercise 8

The Internment of Japanese American Citizens:
The Bill of Rights Outside of the Fence
and Inside of the Fence

Note to the Teacher:

When Madison was drafting the Bill of Rights, he was concerned that principles of personal liberty would be violated in a time of crisis and sought to reduce that possibility. For all his care, violations have occurred. One of the cases affecting the most people was the internment of American citizens of Japanese descent during World War II. Measures taken by the executive, legislative, and judicial branches deprived these citizens of their constitutional rights. What the government denied, these citizens reaffirmed through their actions behind the barbed wire fence. Within the limits of their confinement, they attempted to exercise rights and reconstitute democratic institutions to govern their daily lives.

Prior to the outbreak of war, the Federal Bureau of Investigation had identified German, Italian, and Japanese aliens who were suspected of being potential enemy agents. Following Pearl Harbor, the West Coast was divided into military zones and suspect enemy aliens were kept under surveillance. By mid-January 1942, demands arose to exclude not only suspicious aliens whose origins were in belligerent nations, but all persons of Japanese descent, whether foreign born (issei) or American citizens (nisei).

Pressure on Congress was generated by interest groups from the western states, which included some associations of fruit and vegetable growers, veterans' groups, labor unions, and white supremacy groups. During congressional committee hearings, representatives of the Department of Justice raised logistical, constitutional, and ethical objections to the proposal, so the task was turned over to the U.S. Army as a security matter, despite the practical and legal reservations of some military commanders.

On February 19, 1942, President Franklin D. Roosevelt issued Executive Order 9066 (**document 32**) authorizing military commanders to exclude civilians from military areas. Although the language of the order did not specify any ethnic group, Lieutenant General John L. DeWitt of the Western Defense Command proceeded to announce curfews that included only Japanese Americans. Next, he encouraged voluntary evacuation by Japanese Americans from a limited number of areas; about 7 percent of the total Japanese American population in these areas complied. On March 29, 1942, under the authority of the executive order, DeWitt issued Public Proclamation No. 4, which began the controlled, involuntary evacuation and detention of West Coast residents of Japanese American ancestry on a 48-hour notice. Only a few days prior to the posting of DeWitt's proclamation, on March 21, Congress had passed Public Law 503 (**document 33**), which made violation of Executive Order 9066 a misdemeanor punishable by up to one year in prison and a $5,000 fine. From the end of March to August, approximately 112,000 persons left their homes for civil control stations, proceeded to assembly centers, then were transported to relocation centers across the interior of the country (**document 34**). Nearly 70,000 of the evacuees were American citizens. There were no charges of disloyalty against any of these citizens, nor was there any vehicle by which they could appeal their loss of property and personal liberty.

The government's actions were challenged in three major cases, the most significant of which was *Korematsu v. United States*. Fred Korematsu was a nisei who wished to join the Army and fight America's foes. He eluded internment by going into hiding, but he was caught, tried, and convicted under Public Law 503. He received 5 years probation and was sent to the Topaz, UT, relocation center. His lawyers, from the American Civil Liberties Union, appealed the case to the Supreme Court. On December 18, 1944, the court rendered its judgment (**document 35**). In a 6-3 decision, the Supreme Court denied Korematsu's appeal, rejecting his lawyers' argument that he had been unconstitutionally deprived of his rights because of his race. The Court instead upheld the legality of the evacuation order, stating,

Korematsu was not excluded from the Military Area because of hostility to him or his race. He was excluded because we are at war with the Japanese Empire, because the properly constituted military authorities feared an invasion of our West Coast and felt constrained to take proper security measures, because they decided that the military urgency of the situation demanded that all citizens of Japanese ancestry be segregated from the West Coast temporarily, and finally, because Congress, reposing its confidence in this time of war in our military leaders – as inevitably it must – determined that they should have the power to do just this.

The decision continues to stand after more than 40 years and remains the legal precedent for evacuation by the government.

The role of the public cannot be minimized in these events. Voices advocating internment were well organized and spoke persuasively to a shocked citizenry's fear of sabotage, espionage, and fifth column support for Japanese troops that they conjectured might be perpetrated by Japanese Americans loyal to the emperor. Walter Lippmann published a column (**document 37**) articulating these concerns the week before Executive Order 9066 was proclaimed. Other advocates spoke of internment as protective custody, saving the Japanese Americans from vigilantes. Those who opposed internment included church groups, some social services workers, civil liberties groups, and Edward J. Ennis, head of the Department of Justice's Alien Enemy Control Unit. A petition from the Presbytery of the Redwoods (**document 36**) anticipated the arguments raised by Korematsu's lawyers by questioning how American citizens can be denied due process of law.

The relocation camps were created and sustained by the full authority of the government, so no recourse was left other than compliance. The Japanese Americans were interned in fenced relocation camps (**document 38**), issei and nisei alike (**document 39**). Yet, even the smallest details of life in the United States were duplicated; in one Heart Mountain report, it was noted that the Girl Scouts had completely sold out their supply of cookies. More significantly, democratic institutions and personal rights were painstakingly replicated in the camps. Internees held block meetings, elected representatives to the camp councils, established rules of conduct, enforced those rules, and judged offenders. Records from the War Relocation Authority show how democratic rights fared in the face of adversity. Testimony from Heart Mountain, WY, includes two pages from the February 1943 quarterly report prepared by the camp council for the War Relocation Authority (**documents 40** and **41**) and an issue of the *Heart Mountain Buddhist's Digest* (**document 42**). The Hunt High School student government pages (**document 43**) from Minidoka, ID, and an interview with a student relocation counselor (**document 44**) at Topaz, UT, focus on students' hopes and concerns.

Ironically, while nisei were deprived of their rights as citizens, they were held to the citizens' responsibility of fighting in wartime. More than 30,000 Japanese Americans served in both theaters during World War II.

For additional information related to Japanese American internment and a document-based lesson plan online, visit the Digital Classroom at the National Archives Web site at **www.nara.gov/education** and click on the Constitution Community.

Time: 2 class periods

Objectives:

- To examine the constitutional impact of Japanese American internment.

- To demonstrate an understanding of the interrelationship of a group of documents.

Materials Needed:

Documents 32-44
Photograph Analysis worksheet, p. 14
Worksheet 7

Procedures:

1. The National Archives is charged with preserving the permanently valuable records of the U.S. government. Archivists are required to appraise (evaluate) documents to decide if they will be kept. Divide the class into five groups, then distribute five sets of documents 32-44 to each group. Assign students to write an appraisal report for each of the 13 documents. Students should consider the circumstances surrounding the creation of the document, its research value, its legal value, and its intrinsic value (the value the document may have because of its rarity, historical significance, the signatures it bears, or its appearance). Take some time to explain what these terms mean. In addition, students should develop a list of points archivists might also consider when appraising documents. Ask each group to share one or two major findings with the entire class.

2. During the group work, instruct each student to review document 41, the photograph, and complete the Photograph Analysis worksheet.

3. Provide each student with a copy of document 38 and "Mending Wall" by Robert Frost and direct them to read the essay and poem and then select a writing assignment from the following suggestions. (You may wish to substitute the lyrics of Cole Porter's song, "Don't Fence Me In," for the poem in this exercise.)

   a. On the night of November 17, 1943, an ode party was held at Recreation Hall 20 at Topaz, UT. As one of the women who attended the ode party that evening, what did you write?

   b. If you had drafted the petition from Heart Mountain, WY, that was sent to Washington asking that no fence be erected, what would you have said?

   c. Assume the role of the M.P. standing sentry duty on the Heart Mountain watch tower. Write a diary entry on the day you took the jeep out and arrested women who had gone outside of the fence to pick wire out of lettuce crates for making artificial flowers.

4. Duplicate and distribute worksheet 7 and ask students to complete it by evaluating whether evidence in the documents indicates that the Bill of Rights provisions listed were denied, exercised by, or not applicable to Japanese Americans, outside of the fence and inside of the fence, and citing the number of the supporting documents. In the cases where there is insufficient evidence in the documents to make a decision, instruct students to write "insufficient."

5. Extended activities:

   a. Ask several of the students to conduct further research about the Japanese American internment to find evidence to evaluate the sections of worksheet 7 that were marked insufficient and to share their findings with the class.

   b. Ask one student to use periodicals or Web sources to investigate the Civil Liberties Act of 1988 and report the current status of Japanese American claims. (Information available online at the Department of Justice Web site in the Civil Rights Division, **www.usdoj.gov**.)

   c. If possible, invite someone in your community who lived in a relocation camp to visit your classroom and tell your students about her or his experience.

   d. *Korematsu* still stands as a precedent. Ask students if they can foresee any case where history might repeat itself.

Exercise 8: The Internment of Japanese American Citizens

Worksheet 7

Directions: Evaluate documents 32-44 to decide if there is evidence in the documents that indicate that the Bill of Rights provisions listed were denied, exercised by, or not applicable to Japanese Americans. Cite the number of the supporting document(s). If there is not enough evidence to make a decision, write "insufficient."

The Bill of Rights	Outside the Fence	Inside the Fence
1. religion		
speech		
press		
assembly		
petition		
2. bear arms		
3. quarter troops		
4. search & seizure of persons, houses, papers & effects		
5. no detention without an indictment		
double jeopardy		
self incrimination		
due process to deprive of life,		
liberty,		
property		
compensation for seized property		
6. speedy, public trial		
trial by impartial jury		
inform of charges		
confront accuser		
witnesses for defense		
counsel		
7. trial by jury in suits over $20		
8. excessive bail & fines		
cruel & unusual punishment		
9. rights retained by people		
10. powers reserved by states		

Exercise 9
Individual Rights and the Common Good

Note to the Teacher:

In the opinion for *Weems v. United States*, the Supreme Court observed,

> Time works changes, brings into existence new conditions and purposes. Therefore a principle to be vital must be capable of wider application than the mischief which gave it birth .... In the application of a constitution, therefore, our contemplation cannot be only of what has been but of what may be. Under any other rule a constitution would indeed be as easy of application as it would be deficient in efficacy and power. Its general principles would have little value and be converted by precedent into lifeless and impotent formulas. Rights declared in words might be lost in reality.

The 20th century has brought with it sophisticated technologies and an expanded role for government – developments that challenge principles framed in the 18th century. Through legislation, executive action, judicial interpretation, and citizens' exercise of rights, Americans have attempted to adapt the Bill of Rights to new circumstances. The ongoing tension between individual rights and the general welfare has provided opportunity for resolving conflicts between rights and for defining new, emerging rights.

On March 29, 1960, the *New York Times* published an advertisement (**document 45**) placed by the Committee to Defend Martin Luther King and the Struggle for Freedom in the South. Police Commissioner L. B. Sullivan of Montgomery, AL, sued the newspaper, claiming the advertisement was libelous and the paper was negligent in publishing it. Sullivan's lawyers argued that the misstatements and errors in the advertisement, although impersonal, nonetheless libeled Sullivan in his role as a government official. A jury in Montgomery awarded him $500,000 in damages, an action that the Supreme Court of Alabama affirmed. When the *New York Times* appealed to the Supreme Court of the United States, the justices had to decide whether free speech and press, in this case a common good, had precedence over protection from libel, an intensely personal right. On March 9, 1964, Justice William J. Brennan delivered the opinion of the Court in favor of the *New York Times*, ruling that freedom of expression was the paramount issue in this case. The decision of the Alabama courts had transformed impersonal criticism of government into personal, potentially libelous criticism. In uncompromising words, Brennan rejected the proposition.

> Raising as it does the possibility that a good-faith critic of government will be penalized for his criticism, the proposition relied on by the Alabama courts strikes at the very center of the constitutionally protected area of free expression. We hold that such a proposition may not constitutionally be utilized to establish that an otherwise impersonal attack on governmental operations was a libel of an official responsible for those operations.

A different conflict between individual and society comes from rapid technological progress. Technology, from wiretaps to shared databases, has increased the ability of government to collect information on citizens at a time when increasing amounts of information are available. In the face of this new situation, government and citizens are groping to define rights of privacy and of access to information. Drawing from the First, Third, Fourth, and Ninth Amendments, these rights are, at this time, only partially articulated. Freedom of personal belief and access to information upon which belief may be formed are well defined. Privacy of the home is assured by the proscription of quartering and unreasonable search and seizure. However, the question of the degree to which the government can intrude into aspects of private life, from sodomy laws to involuntary, random drug testing, remains unresolved. The degree of access to information the government considers private for security reasons is also being redefined.

In 1966, Congress passed S. 1160 (**document 46**), entitled the Freedom of Information Act (FOIA), which took effect July 4, 1967. The FOIA is a disclosure statute granting access to final opinions and orders of agencies, policy statements, interpretations, and other executive department records affecting members of the public. It does not cover records created by Congress or the federal courts. Exemptions made to protect the common welfare include national security classified files, personnel files, records of ongoing criminal investigations, and several other specific categories of files. Amendments to the FOIA were enacted over the veto of President Ford in 1974 and took effect on February 19, 1975.

The Federal Privacy Act was passed and became effective on September 27, 1975. This act has a different focus from the FOIA since it covers records retrievable by personal identifiers such as name or social security number. It also provides safeguards for an individual against an invasion of personal privacy and permits an individual to determine what records the government may have collected, maintained, or disseminated on him or her. Further, it allows citizens to request correction of erroneous records.

Although the amended FOIA and the Privacy Act address different aspects of access to government information, together they have helped articulate the public's right to privacy and to information.

Time: 2 or 3 class periods

Objectives:

* To examine a case involving conflict between personal liberties and the common good.

* To identify the major provisions of the Freedom of Information Act.

Materials Needed:

Documents 45 and 46

Procedures:

1. In preparation for using document 45, post the advertisement in the classroom and ask students to read it over the next several days.

2. Take down the advertisement and read aloud the first paragraph. Then, pass the document to a student to read the second paragraph, then to another student to read the third paragraph, and so on. When they have completed reading the text of the advertisement, ask them the following questions.

   a. How did you feel when you heard this?

   b. How do you think the editors of the *New York Times* felt when they accepted this ad?

   c. How do you think the police commissioner of Montgomery, AL, felt when he read this ad?

   Read through the names at the bottom of the advertisement. Ask students if any of the names are familiar and, if so, in what context.

3. Divide the class into four groups.

   a. **Press Ethics Group:** Students are to make an in-depth study of the issues related to ethical standards for the press and compile a code of ethics for their operation. Ask the students to prepare a debate on the best means for implementing the code. One student should act as a moderator, with one or two students arguing the pro side and one or two the con side of the issue, "Resolved: The government should adopt legislation establishing a code of ethics for the press and an agency to enforce adherence to such a code." At the conclusion of the argument, the audience should be asked to vote their agreement or disagreement with the resolution.

b. **Newspaper Group:** Ask the students of this group to contact a local newspaper and find out from the editor if the paper has a code of ethics or a review procedure for stories to protect citizens from abuse. Oral reports on their findings should be presented to the class.

c. **Radio Group:** Ask the students of this group to contact a local radio station and find out from the station manager if it has a code of ethics or other review policies about stories it airs. To what government regulations must it conform in order to have its license renewed? If there is more than one station in the area, students should contact one or two other stations to see if different procedures are followed by different stations. Oral reports on their findings should be presented to the class.

d. **Television Group:** Ask the students of this group to contact a local television station or stations and find out from the station manager if the station has a code of ethics or review procedures to evaluate the news and programs it airs. To what government regulations must the station conform in order to continue broadcasting? Oral reports on their findings should be presented to the class.

4. Duplicate and distribute copies of document 46 to the students. Assign students to read the document, to outline its contents, and to answer the following questions as homework.

a. What provisions of the bill ensure public access to government information?

b. What provisions of the bill ensure personal privacy?

c. What provisions of the bill ensure national security?

d. Does this bill protect personal rights more than national security?

e. Is this act useful to you today? What might its value be to you 10 years from now?

This Act was subsequently amended. The Government Printing Office published the House Committee on Government Operations' July 1, 1987, report called *A Citizen's Guide on Using the Freedom of Information Act and the Privacy Act of 1974 to Request Government Documents, 13th Report,* 052-071-00752-1. This inexpensive, 56-page document contains updated information about amendments to FOIA, a sample letter for making a FOIA request, and other helpful suggestions. For a current version of this Act go to the Government Printing Office Web site at **www.gpo.gov** and search for Freedom of Information Act or conduct a search on the Act at **www.firstgov.gov**.

Exercise 10
Summary Exercise: The Bill of Rights

Note to the Teacher:

Inherent in any democracy is the potential for the majority to tyrannize a minority. In the United States, the Bill of Rights provides checks and balances to protect individual rights from governmental excess. It is a written enjoinder that compels the government to uphold our most cherished rights. It does not attempt to list every aspiration and hope of humanity; such specific lists have proved to be invariably incomplete and largely unenforceable. Instead, the U.S. Bill of Rights identifies rights that a majoritarian government might be tempted to abridge and unequivocally declares them inviolable. "Congress shall make no law . . ." and "No State shall make or enforce any law . . ." are surprisingly blunt, unaccommodating phrases in a constitution born of compromise. Such wording guarantees minorities a mechanism for challenging the establishment. The Bill of Rights gives few definitions, thereby enabling rights and values to evolve.

While it is important to look at rights individually, the following procedures challenge students to consider the Bill of Rights as a whole, how it has evolved, what its successes and limitations have been, how it compares with guarantees by other political systems, and finally, into what areas it may be extended in the future.

Time: Flexible

Objectives:

- To demonstrate an understanding of the interrelationship of the documents as a group.

- To compare and contrast the U.S. Bill of Rights with other countries' safeguards of rights.

- To project probable trends in the future for the Bill of Rights.

Materials Needed:

Documents 1-46

Procedures:

1. Discuss with the class this question: It has been said that no easy problem reaches the Oval Office. It is equally true that no simple questions are argued before the Supreme Court. This can, in part, be attributed to the appellate procedures established by Congress and the emphasis on process in the Constitution, the Bill of Rights, and the Fourteenth Amendment. Yet, without a philosophy of government that supports review, the mechanisms of the judiciary would be idle. What explicit and implicit ideals in the Constitution and Bill of Rights propel these difficult problems forward to the Supreme Court?

2. As an in-depth research activity:

    a. Ask students to go to a university or legal library and examine *United States Supreme Court Reports* for a list of the cases that were on the 1887 docket of the Supreme Court. Ask them to identify and list the major issues that preoccupied the Court at the time of the Constitution's centennial.

    b. Then, ask students to get a list of the cases that were on the 1987 docket of the Supreme Court. Instruct them to identify and list the major issues that preoccupied the Court at the time of the Constitution's bicentennial. Ask them to compare and contrast this list with the 1887 list and account for differences.

    c. Finally, ask students to project what issues will preoccupy the Court in 2087 for the tricentennial of the Constitution.

3. Much of the impetus for a bill of rights comes from the English tradition under Magna Carta and the 1688 bill of rights. There is, however, no written bill to uphold rights in Great Britain, simply the common law tradition. Ask students to compare and contrast the protection of rights in contemporary Britain with those in the United States. Specific areas of inquiry might include:

    a. freedom of the press to report on security matters;

    b. freedom of religion and an established Church of England;

    c. rights of the accused, especially in Northern Ireland under British internment policies.

4. Many countries have comprehensive bills of rights, Russia among them. Ask the students to obtain copies of the bill of rights of other nations and to compare and contrast the contents with that of the United States. Ask them to investigate enforcement of the selected nations' bills of rights. Discuss with your students the benefits and limitations of extensive expressed rights.

5. Lead the class in a discussion of the question: What rights would you want to see added to the Bill of Rights in the next 50 years? Justify these additions from the point of view of the individual and from that of the public.

6. If possible, coordinate with teachers in other disciplines to devote time during their class periods on one day or during one week to examine how the Bill of Rights touches on their subjects. For example, a French teacher may want to look at how the Bill of Rights influenced the French Declaration of the Rights of Man. An English teacher may want to focus on censorship by having students read and discuss John Milton's *Areopagitica*. In computer science classes the problems of databases and privacy might be considered. In biology, the tension between the medical procedures available to patients and rights of the elderly to death with dignity or rights of the unborn could be explored. The question of mandatory drug testing of athletes would be suitable for physical education or health classes.

Transcription of Document 2

State of Rhode Island

At a Town Meeting of the Freemen of the Town of Providence, holden by Adjournment at the State House in Providence on the 3d Day of July 1779

Whereas many of the Inhabitants of this Town, have been at great Expense and have suffered much on account of the Troops having been Barracked upon the Inhabitants Since the Enemy have been in Possession of Rhode Island: and As the whole Community of the United States are Equally concerned in and benefited by the War and as far as may be ought Equally to Bear and Support the Burthen thereof, and it is Right and Just that the Expense of Providing Barracks for the Troops should be defrayed and borne by the Public in General:

It is therefore Voted and Resolved that Nicholas Brown Esq. Ephraim Bowen Esq. and James Mitchel Varnum Esq. be and they hereby are appointed a committee to draft a letter on this Subject to the Delegates in Congress from this State representing the Situation of the Town and requesting them to use their Endeavour that Barracks be provided at the Expense of the United States for the Accomodation of the Troops in case it shall be necessary that any be Quartered on this Town the approaching Winter

A True Copy

Attest   Theodore Foster   Town Clerk

Time Line

June 15, 1215	King John signs Magna Carta.
May 28, 1628	Parliament passes the English Petition of Right.
December 10, 1641	Massachusetts adopts the Body of Liberties.
April 25, 1682	Pennsylvania adopts its Frame of Government with a listing of rights.
December 16, 1689	King William and Queen Mary accept the 1688 English Bill of Rights.
February 10, 1763	Treaty of Paris ends the French and Indian War.
March 24, 1765	Quartering Act goes into effect in the British North American colonies.
October 19, 1765	The Stamp Act Congress issues its Declaration of Rights and Grievances.
March 5, 1770	Colonists and British soldiers clash during the Boston Massacre.
December 16, 1773	Colonists disguised as Mohawk Indians dump taxable tea into Boston harbor during the Boston Tea Party.
October 14, 1774	The First Continental Congress passes the Declaration of Rights **(document 1)**.
April 19, 1775	The Revolutionary War begins with fighting at Lexington and Concord.
July 4, 1776	Declaration of Independence is adopted.
July 3, 1779	Providence, RI, town meeting requests that the U.S. government build barracks for Continental troops **(document 2)**.
October 19, 1781	General Cornwallis surrenders at Yorktown.
January 16, 1786	Virginia adopts the Statute for Religious Freedom.
September 14, 1787	George Mason, Elbridge Gerry, and Charles Pinckney unsuccessfully attempt to have a bill of rights added to the Constitution.
September 17, 1787	Delegates to the Constitutional Convention approve the Constitution.
August 1, 1788	North Carolina rejects the Constitution and sends to Congress a proposed bill of rights **(document 3)**.
April 1, 1789	The House of Representatives opens the first session of the First Congress.
April 30, 1789	George Washington is inaugurated in New York City as the first President of the United States.
June 8, 1789	James Madison proposes nine amendments to enlarge the Constitution to eight articles.
July 21, 1789	Madison reintroduces the subject of a bill of rights, which is sent to committee.
August 21, 1789	The House of Representatives approves 17 amendments **(document 4)**.
September 9, 1789	The Senate passes 12 amendments.
September 19, 1789	A House-Senate conference committee takes up the 12 amendments.
September 24, 1789	The House adopts the conference report's 12 amendments.

September 24, 1789	The Senate adopts the conference report's 12 amendments.
September 28, 1789	Speaker of the House Frederick Muhlenberg signs the enrolled original of the Bill of Rights **(document 5)**.
December 15, 1791	Virginia's ratification adds 10 amendments, called the Bill of Rights, to the Constitution **(document 6)**.
March 1, 1792	Thomas Jefferson, Secretary of State, announces ratification of 10 amendments in a circular letter to governors of the states.
March 4, 1797	John Adams is inaugurated as President.
June 25, 1798	Congress passes the Alien Act.
July 14, 1798	Congress passes the Sedition Act.
December 24, 1798	Virginia Resolutions condemn the Alien and Sedition Acts.
November 16 and 22, 1799	Kentucky Resolutions condemn the Alien and Sedition Acts.
April 1800	Thomas Cooper is indicted for libel under the Sedition Act.
March 3, 1801	The Sedition Act expires.
March 3, 1820	Congress passes the Missouri Compromise.
February 24, 1825	A House committee reports on Thomas Cooper's petition **(document 14)**.
February 16, 1833	John Marshall renders a decision in *Barron v. Baltimore*.
March 6, 1836	Mexican troops capture the Alamo.
February 2, 1848	Treaty of Guadalupe Hidalgo ends the Mexican War.
September 9-20, 1850	The Senate debates and works out the Compromise of 1850.
November 6, 1860	Abraham Lincoln is elected President.
April 12, 1861	The Civil War begins with the bombardment of Fort Sumter, SC.
April 7, 1862	General Grant commands Union troops at the battle of Shiloh.
December 17, 1862	General Grant issues General Order No. 11.
January 5, 1863	Senator Lazarus W. Powell introduces a resolution condemning General Order No. 11 **(document 12)**.
July 1-3, 1863	Battle rages around Gettysburg.
April 9, 1865	General Lee surrenders to General Grant at Appomattox.
June 16, 1866	The Fourteenth Amendment is submitted to states for ratification **(document 7)**.
May 13, 1870	The Supreme Court allows the writ of error in the first Slaughterhouse case **(document 8)**.
September 29, 1871	H.C. Whitley reports on Ku Klux Klan activities **(document 9)**.
January 19, 1874	Cleveland, TN, citizens petition for enforcement of the Fourteenth Amendment **(document 10)**.
April 24, 1877	Federal troops withdraw from Louisiana, the last occupied southern state, ending Reconstruction.

May 18, 1896	*Plessy v. Ferguson* establishes the doctrine of "separate but equal."
February 15, 1898	U.S.S. *Maine* blows up in Havana harbor, precipitating the Spanish-American War.
February 24, 1907	A Gentleman's Agreement is concluded between the United States and Japan ending segregation of Japanese students by San Francisco schools in exchange for voluntary immigration restrictions by Japan.
August 15, 1914	The Panama Canal opens.
September 11, 1916	The Federal Child Labor Law is adopted.
April 6, 1917	The United States enters World War I.
June 15, 1917	The Espionage Act becomes law (**document 15**).
November 12, 1917	*Los Angeles Daily Times* publishes an article on the government's waste of energy (**document 16**).
May 15, 1918	A Jehovah's Witnesses' book, *The Finished Mystery*, is restricted under the Espionage Act (**document 17**).
May 16, 1918	The Sedition Act becomes law.
March 3, 1919	*Schenck v. United States* decision upholds the constitutionality of the Espionage Act.
August 5, 1919	The postmistress of Melbourne, FL, seizes a poster of a black soldier's family under the Espionage Act (**document 18**).
December 3, 1923	The proposed child labor amendment is sent to the states for ratification (**document 27**).
June 8, 1925	*Gitlow v. New York* decision nationalizes the free expression clause of the First Amendment.
November 6, 1925	An Ohio judge sends a letter to the Supreme Court inquiring about the *Gitlow* decision (**document 19**).
June 4, 1928	The practice of wiretapping is upheld in the case of *Olmstead v. United States*.
October 24, 1929	The stock market crashes.
November 8, 1932	Franklin D. Roosevelt is elected President for the first time.
September 1, 1939	Adolf Hitler invades Poland, starting World War II.
December 7, 1941	Japanese forces attack Pearl Harbor, HI, prompting the entry of the United States into World War II.
February 12, 1942	Walter Lippman's fifth-column article is published (**document 37**).
February 19, 1942	President Roosevelt issues Executive Order 9066 (**document 32**).
March 21, 1942	Public Law 503 takes effect (**document 33**).
April 15, 1942	The Presbytery of the Redwoods petitions Congress to reconsider the Japanese-American evacuation (**document 36**).
November 1942	Heart Mountain Quarterly Report is issued (**documents 39, 41**).
February 19, 1943	Estelle Ishigo paints a watercolor of Heart Mountain for the Quarterly Report (**document 40**).

June 5, 1943	General John L. DeWitt issues the *Final Report of Western Defense Command* (**document 34**).
June 14, 1943	The Supreme Court issues its mandate for *West Virginia v. Barnette* on Flag Day (**document 13**).
July 7, 1943	The Buddhist church of Heart Mountain, WY, publishes its weekly journal (**document 42**).
August 11, 1943	An evacuee writes "The Fence" (**document 38**).
April 1944	An interview with the student relocation counselor at Topaz, UT, is reported (**document 44**).
1944	Hunt High School publishes *Memoirs*, the high school yearbook for Minidoka, ID (**document 43**).
December 18, 1944	The Supreme Court announces its opinion in *Korematsu v. United States* (**document 35**).
August 14, 1945	V-J Day.
November 14, 1946	The ACLU files an amicus curiae brief in the *Everson* case (**document 11**).
December 1, 1955	Rosa Parks is arrested in Montgomery, AL.
April 2, 1956	President Eisenhower issues the Child Health Day proclamation (**document 28**).
October 4, 1957	The Soviet Union launches *Sputnik I*.
September 2, 1958	The National Defense Education Act becomes law (**document 29**).
February 2, 1960	Sit-ins begin at Woolworth's lunch counter in Greensboro, NC.
March 29, 1960	The *New York Times* publishes the Committee to Defend Martin Luther King and the Struggle for Freedom in the South's advertisement (**document 45**).
April 19, 1962	Clarence Earl Gideon responds to the respondent's response to his petition for a writ of certiorari (**document 23**).
November 22, 1963	Lee Harvey Oswald assassinates President John F. Kennedy.
December 18, 1963	The attorney for the Bureau of Alcohol, Tobacco and Firearms sends a letter to Senator Warren Magnuson about firearms control (**document 22**).
June 15, 1964	Judge McGhee issues an order for the commitment of Gerald Gault to state reformatory school (**document 30**).
August 2, 1964	U.S.S. *Maddox* is attacked in the Gulf of Tonkin.
October 4, 1965	Freedom of Information bill is introduced before the House (**document 46**).
July 13, 1965	Ernesto Miranda files an affidavit in forma pauperis (**document 24**).
July 25, 1966	John Tinker testifies at his trial (**document 20**).
August 11, 1967	A Chatham County, GA, grand jury indicts William Furman on the charge of murder (**document 25**).
September 20, 1968	A Chatham County, GA, jury convicts Furman of murder, and the presiding judge sentences him to death (**document 25**).
October 31, 1968	The Smothers Brothers write a letter of apology to President Lyndon B. Johnson (**document 21**).
August 8, 1974	Richard Nixon resigns the office of the President of the United States.

January 22, 1975	The Supreme Court rules in the case of *Goss v. Lopez* (**document 31**).
April 30, 1975	The United States withdraws from South Vietnam as Saigon falls.
November 4, 1980	Ronald Reagan is elected President.
February 1, 1984	The U.S. Senate Republican Policy Committee publishes a *Legislative Notice* regarding S. 1765 (**document 26**).

October 31, 1968

The President
The White House
Washington, D.C.

Mr. President:

During the past couple of years we have taken satirical
jabs at you and more than occasionally overstepped our
bounds. We disregarded the respect due the office and
the tremendous burden of running the country because of
our own emotional feelings regarding the war. We frequently disregarded the many, many good works and the
progress the country has made under your administration.

We saw the television broadcast you made last night in
behalf of the Democratic Party and Hubert Humphrey and
were quite moved by your sincerity and by the content
of the message. If the opportunity arose in this coming
election to vote for you, we would.

Often an emotional issue such as the war makes people
tend to over-react. Please accept our apology on behalf
of the Smothers Brothers Comedy Hour for our over-
reaction in some instances. Please know that we do
admire what you have done for the country and particularly your dignity in accepting the abuses of so many people.

We are now working for the election of Hubert Humphrey
and much of the enthusiasm we have for him is due to
that broadcast of yours.

We just saw your message on Viet Nam and with all America,
are pleased at your determined move to halt the bombing
in an effort to achieve peace.

Respectfully,

Tom Smothers

Dick Smothers

Table of Cases

Barron v. Baltimore, 32 U.S. (7 Pet.) 243 (1833)

Butchers Benevolent Association of New Orleans v. The Crescent City Live-stock Landing and Slaughter House Company, 16 Wallace 36, 21 L. Ed. 394 (1873)

Betts v. Brady, 316 U.S. 455 (1942)

Bridges v. California, 314 U.S. 252 (1941)

Escobedo v. Illinois 378 U.S. 478, 84 S. Ct. 1758, 12 L. Ed. 2d 977 (1964)

Everson v. Board of Education of Ewing Township, New Jersey, 330 U.S. 1, 67 S. Ct. 504, 91 L. Ed. 711 (1947)

Furman v. Georgia, 408 U.S. 238, 92 S. Ct. 2726, 33 L. Ed. 2d 346 (1972)

Gideon v. Wainright, 372 U.S. 335, 83 S. Ct. 792, 9 L. Ed. 2d 799 (1963)

Gitlow v. New York, 268 U.S. 652, 45 S. Ct. 625, 69 L. Ed. 1138 (1925)

Goss v. Lopez, 419 U.S. 565, 95 S. Ct. 729, 94 L. Ed. 2d 725 (1975)

in re Gault, 387 U.S. 1, 87 S. Ct. 1428, 18 L. Ed. 2d 527 (1967)

Korematsu v. United States, 323 U.S. 214 (1944)

Malloy v. Hogan, 378 U.S. 1, 84 S. Ct. 1489, 12 L. Ed. 2d 653 (1964)

Miranda v. Arizona, 384 U.S. 436, 86 S. Ct. 1602, 16 L. Ed. 2d 694 (1966)

New York Times Co. v. Sullivan, 376 U.S. 254, 84 S. Ct. 710, 11 L. Ed. 2d 686 (1964)

Olmstead v. United States, 277 U.S. 438 (1928)

Plessy v. Ferguson, 163 U.S. 537, 16 S. Ct. 1138, 41 L. Ed. 256 (1896)

Powell v. Alabama, 287 U.S. 45 (1932)

Presser v. Illinois, 116 U.S. 252 (1886)

Schenck v. United States, 249 U.S. 47, 39 S. Ct. 247, 6 L. Ed. 470 (1919)

Thomas v. Collins, 323 U.S. 516 (1945)

Tinker v. Des Moines Independent Community School District, 393 U.S. 503, 89 S. Ct. 733, 21 L. Ed. 2d 731 (1969)

United States v. Cruikshank, 92 U.S. 542 (1876)

United States v. Miller, 307 U.S. 174 (1939)

Weems v. United States, 217 U.S. 349 (1910)

West Virginia State Board of Education v. Barnette, 319 U.S. 624 (1943)

Annotated Bibliography

Amnesty International. *USA: The Death Penalty, Briefing*. London: Amnesty International Publications, 1987.

> A collection of articles highly critical of the death penalty in the United States. Included are good statistical tables of information about the death penalty. Suitable for secondary students; teachers guide also available.

Arbetman, Lee; Roe, Richard L.; and David, Andrew. *Great Trials in American History, Civil War to the Present*. St. Paul, MN: West Pub. Co., 1997.

> Short chapters chronicle the stories behind the major civil liberties trials from the Scottsboro cases to Gault. Suitable for secondary students; teachers guide also available.

Baker, Livia. *Miranda, Crime, Law and Politics*. New York: Atheneum, 1983.

> Exhaustively researched examination of the case of Ernesto Miranda and the behind-the-scenes politics between the executive and judicial branches that culminated in this landmark decision. Suitable for highly motivated students and teachers.

Brant, Irving. *The Bill of Rights*. Indianapolis: The Bobbs-Merrill Co., 1965.

> Tracing the origins of rights from English law and colonial protest, Brant continues by examining events, such as the Alien and Sedition Acts, which restricted or extended guarantees of personal liberty in America. Well written and informative for both high school students and teachers.

_____. *James Madison: Father of the Constitution, 1787-1800*. New York: Bobbs-Merrill Co., Inc., 1950.

> One of six volumes on the life of James Madison. Traces Madison's evolving attitudes toward a bill of rights. Well written and readable for students and teachers.

Claude, Richard P. *Comparative Human Rights*. Baltimore: The Johns Hopkins University Press, 1976.

> Fifteen essays explore rights from a comparative, international point of view. First Amendment rights, due process, and the rights of minors are examined in a cross-cultural context. Suitable for motivated high school students and teachers.

Cohen, William, and Kaplan, John. *The Bill of Rights, Constitutional Law for Undergraduates*. Mineola, NY: The Foundation Press, Inc., 1976.

> A case book for Constitutional law that focuses specifically and by implication on the individual freedoms set out in the Bill of Rights. Suitable for teachers.

Commission on Wartime Relocation and Internment of Civilians. *Personal Justice Denied*. Washington, DC: Civil Liberties Public Education Fund ; Seattle: University of Washington Press, 1997.

> The most recent study by the government of its wartime policy of internment of Japanese-American citizens. Excellent background information for teachers.

Cortner, Richard C. *The Supreme Court and the Second Bill of Rights: The 14th Amendment and the Nationalization of Civil Liberties*. Madison, WI: University of Wisconsin Press, 1981.

> Examines the Supreme Court's interpretations of the Fourteenth Amendment that led to the nationalization of the Bill of Rights. Suitable for teachers.

Cress, Lawrence Delbert. "A Well-regulated Militia." *This Constitution* 14 (Spring 1987): 21-23.

> A brief examination of the bearing of the militia on the adoption of the Second Amendment. Suitable for students and teachers.

Cushman, Robert F., ed. *Leading Constitutional Decisions.* 18th ed. Englewood Cliffs, NJ: Prentice Hall, 1992.

In this edition, Cushman provides a useful, extensive introduction for Supreme Court cases representing the evolution of ideas pertaining to the three federal branches, nationalization of the Bill of Rights, First Amendment rights, rights of the accused, and equal protection of rights. Suitable for high school students in U.S. government or history.

Danovitch, Sylvia. "The Past Recaptured: The Photographic Record of the Internment of Japanese Americans." *Prologue* 12 (Summer 1980): 91-103.

This article offers suggestions for interpreting historical information from photographs and includes a number of superb photographs from the records of the War Relocation Authority. Suitable for secondary students.

DeWitt, General John L. *Final Report: Japanese Evacuation from the West Coast.* Washington, DC: U.S. Government Printing Office, 1942.

A contemporary report of the evacuation of Japanese-Americans from the West Coast that includes maps, charts, and photographs. Suitable for high school students and teachers.

Dougan, Clark. *The Vietnam Experience, 1968.* Boston: Boston Publishing Co., 1983.

Lavishly illustrated account of the debate within the United States over the government's policy in Vietnam. Suitable for secondary students.

Garraty, John A., ed. *Quarrels That Have Shaped the Constitution.* New York: Perennial Library, 1987.

Sixteen historians contributed essays on Supreme Court decisions from the Marshall to Warren benches. The style and scope recommend it for all students above junior high.

Gettleman, Marvin E., et al. *Vietnam and America, A Documented History.* 2d ed., rev. and enl. New York: Grove Press, 1995.

A history of Vietnam with emphasis on U.S. involvement after World War II through the fall of Saigon in 1975. Utilizes government-generated primary sources.

Grodzins, Morton. *Americans Betrayed: Politics and the Japanese Evacuation.* Chicago: University of Chicago Press, 1949.

An orderly examination that holds up well over time of the decision-making process of the legislative, executive, and judicial branches during the evacuation and internment of Japanese-American citizens. Excellent background reading for teachers.

Guggenheim, Martin, and Sussman, Alan. *The Rights of Young People.* New York: Bantam Books, 1985.

The American Civil Liberties Union handbook of childrens' rights ranging from due process to labor. Written specifically for students.

Halbrook, Stephen. *That Every Man Be Armed: The Evolution of a Constitutional Right.* Albuquerque, NM: University of New Mexico Press, 1984.

Traces the colonial antecedents of the right to bear arms and follows interpretations of the Second Amendment by the court and government agencies to the present. Suitable for high school students and teachers.

Hallin, Daniel C. *The "Uncensored War."* Berkeley: University of California Press, 1989.

A detailed account of the government, media, and press in the Vietnam era that draws extensively from the New York Times and network news programs. Suitable for high school students and teachers.

Hamilton, Alexander; Madison, James; and Jay, John. *The Federalist Papers.* (Various editions.)

> Hamilton, Jay, and Madison collaborated on these 85 essays written to urge the Constitution's ratification. Since then, courts have cited their explanations as authoritative comments. Suitable for high school students and teachers.

Hentoff, Nat. *The First Freedom: The Tumultuous History of Free Speech in America.* New York: Delacorte Press, 1988.

> A lively examination of the history of the First Amendment. For secondary students and teachers.

Houston, Jeanne Wakatsuki. *Farewell to Manzanar.* Austin: Holt, Rinehart and Winston, 2000.

> The Japanese-American internment from the point of view of one family. This account was dramatized for television. For secondary students.

Irons, Peter. *Justice At War: The Story of the Japanese American Internment Cases.* Berkeley: University of California Press, 1993.

> Using documents obtained under the Freedom of Information Act, Irons examines the struggle between attorneys of the War and Justice Departments over the internment policy.

Johnson, Donald Bruce, ed. *National Party Platforms: 1840-1976.* 6th ed. Urbana, IL: University of Illinois Press, 1978.

> A compilation of national political parties' platforms from 1840 through 1976. Between editions, supplements are issued to keep the information up to date. See Supplement through 1980 from same press. Suitable for secondary students and teachers.

Levy, Leonard. *Origins of the Fifth Amendment.* Chicago, IL: Ivan R. Dee, 1999.

> A Pulitzer Prize winning account of the British and colonial experiences that culminated in the Fifth Amendment. Suitable for teachers.

Lewis, Anthony. *Gideon's Trumpet.* New York: Vintage Books, 1989.

> The story of Clarence Earl Gideon, which was dramatized as a television movie in 1980 with Henry Fonda playing the role of Gideon. Suitable for high school students and teachers.

Loeb, Robert H. *Crime and Capital Punishment.* Rev. ed., 2d ed. New York: F. Watts, 1986.

> Traces the origins of capital punishment and presents the arguments pro and con. Written specifically for secondary school students.

MacPherson, Myra. *Long Time Passing.* New York: Anchor Books, 1994.

> Tales of the Vietnam war, the protest movement, and the aftermath of Vietnam in the lives of individuals. Based on 500 interviews. Suitable for high school students and teachers.

McMahon, Edward T.; Arbetman, Lee P.; and O'Brien, Edward L. *Street Law.* 3d ed. New York: West Publishing Co., 1986.

> A course book in practical law covering the areas of criminal and juvenile justice, consumer law, housing law, family law, and civil liberties. Written specifically for secondary school students. A companion teachers' guide is also available, which includes case information, teaching suggestions, and fuller legal citations.

Miller, Helen Hill. *George Mason, Gentleman Revolutionary.* Chapel Hill, NC: The University of North Carolina Press, 1975.

> This readable text includes good background on the Mason family, the history of Virginia, and the architecture and customs of the period all woven into an account of Mason's life and his contributions to Virginia and the nation. Appendices include the text of the first draft of the Virginia Declaration of Rights, the printed "Committee Draft of the Virginia Declaration," and the final version. For all students.

Olney, Ross, R., and Olney, Patricia J. *Up Against The Law: Your Legal Rights as a Minor*. New York: E.P. Dutton, 1985.

> Rights of minors in the family, in court, in contracts, and as operators of vehicles. Written specifically for secondary school students.

Perry, Richard L., ed. *Sources of Our Liberties: Documentary Origins of Individual Liberties in the Constitution and the Bill of Rights*. Rev. ed. Chicago: American Bar Foundation, 1978.

> Selective presentation of major charters in the history of rights from Magna Carta to the Bill of Rights. Includes background information along with transcriptions of the charters.

Personal Privacy Protection Study Commission. *Personal Privacy in an Information Society*. Washington, DC: U.S. Government Printing Office, 1977.

> Government report on the many new techniques and appliances for surveillance which may compromise the right to privacy. Good sourcebook of ideas to promote student discussion and research.

Pfeffer, Leo. *Church, State and Freedom*. Rev. ed. Boston: Beacon Press, 1967.

> This single volume provides a comprehensive study of the origins and history of church-state relations in the United States with references to state and federal cases. A superb reference and text for both teachers and advanced students.

Rutland, Robert Allen. *Birth of the Bill of Rights, 1776-1791*. Boston: Northeastern University Press, 1983.

> This history, based on extensive original sources, traces the Bill of Rights from its English and colonial antecedents through ratification. An excellent account of the progress of Madison's amendments through the first Congress. Suitable for high school students and teachers.

Samuels, D. "Computer scan: no place to hide: the information-technology revolution has exacted a steep toll in individual privacy — often without our knowing it." *PC Magazine* 3 (Jan. 14, 1985): 162-167.

> Describes how data can be accumulated from various sources to form a profile of a person when the subject does not know the information is available. Suitable for students and teachers; lends itself to class discussion.

Schnucker, R.V., ed. "Constitutional History for the Schools Project." *Network News Exchange* 12 (Spring 1987): 11-35.

> Excellent background information and teaching strategies for the Alien and Sedition Acts. Also contains transcriptions of the charters of liberties of several colonies. Suitable for teachers.

Schwartz, Bernard. *The Bill of Rights: A Documentary History*, vols. I, II. 1971.

> A comprehensive presentation of the history of the Bill of Rights through documents. The book draws from private manuscript collections, state libraries and archives, the Library of Congress, and the National Archives to reprint early charters of liberties, legislative proceedings, and letters of the founders. The documents range from the English antecedents of the Bill of Rights to the states' ratifications of the Bill of Rights. Includes introductory commentary by the author. Useful reference for advanced students and teachers.

Schwartz, Bernard, ed. *The American Heritage History of the Law in America*. New York: American Heritage Publishing Co., 1974.

> A well-illustrated survey of law in America with special emphasis on the Supreme Court and its interpretations of Bill of Rights issues from Marshall to Burger. Suitable for secondary students.

Shalhope, Robert E. "The Founding Fathers and the Right to Bear Arms: To Keep the People Duly Armed." *This Constitution* 14 (Spring 1987): 18-20.

> This article reviews the original intent of the revolutionaries who drafted the Second Amendment. Much like people of today, they held conflicting views about this right. Suitable for motivated students and teachers.

Starr, Isidore. *The Idea of Liberty, First Amendment Freedoms.* St. Paul, MN: West Publishing Co., 1978.

> A concise examination of leading Supreme Court cases, and the opinions and dissents that have contributed to the current interpretation of First Amendment freedoms.

Trask, David F., ed. *World War I at Home.* New York: John Wiley and Sons, Inc.,1970.

> Collection of short readings divided into three sections: neutrality (1914-17), belligerency (1917-18), and peacemaking (1919-20). The selections were taken from magazines, newspapers, and other publications printed during the war years and cover a variety of topics including civil liberties. Recommended to the teacher who is interested in short readings for high school students.

U.S. Congress, Office of Technology Assessment. *Science, Technology, and the First Amendment.* OTA-CIT-369. Washington, DC: U.S. Government Printing Office, 1988.

> Congressional assessment of the impact of computers, technology, medicine, and science on the First Amendment that outlines government actions to date. Excellent source book for teachers.

IN THE SUPREME COURT OF THE
UNITED STATES

RECEIVED

JUL 16 1965

OFFICE OF THE CLERK
SUPREME COURT, U.S.

ERNESTO A. MIRANDA,

    Petitioner

   v.

STATE OF ARIZONA,

    Respondent

AFFIDAVIT IN
FORMA PAUPERIS

ERNESTO A. MIRANDA, being duly sworn, deposes and says:

1. I am a citizen of the United States.

2. I am the defendant-petitioner in the above-entitled action.

3. The above-entitled action came on for trial before the Superior Court of Maricopa County, Arizona, on the 20th day of June, 1963, and a verdict was returned on said date finding me guilty as charged, upon which judgment was entered.

4. An appeal was taken by petitioner from said judgment to the Supreme Court of Arizona in forma pauperis with the assistance of court appointed counsel.

5. The said court on the 22nd day of April, 1965 rendered a judgment on appeal affirming the judgment of the trial court.

6. I desire to have the decision of the Supreme Court of Arizona reviewed on certiorari by this Court, and my counsel has prepared a

The Bill of Rights:
Evolution of Personal Liberties
Archival Citations of Documents

1. Declaration of Rights, October 14, 1774; Volume 1, Item 1, pp. 44-49; (National Archives Microfilm Publication M247, roll 8); Papers of the Continental Congress, 1774-1789; Records of the Continental and Confederation Congresses and the Constitutional Convention, 1774-1779, Record Group 360; National Archives Building, Washington, DC.

2. Resolution of Providence, RI, to ask Congress for money to quarter troops, July 3, 1779; Volume 23, Item 78, pp.173-174; (National Archives Microfilm Publication M 247, roll 104); Papers of the Continental Congress, 1774-1789; Records of the Continental and Confederation Congresses and the Constitutional Convention, 1774-1789, Record Group 360; National Archives Building, Washington, DC.

3. North Carolina's proposed amendments to the Constitution, August 1, 1778; (National Archives Microfilm Publication M338, roll 1); Certificates of Ratification of the Constitution and the Bill of Rights, Including Related Correspondence and Rejections of Proposed Amendments, 1787-1792; General Records of the U.S. Government, Record Group 11; National Archives Building, Washington, DC.

4. House journal recording of the 17 amendments proposed for a bill of rights, August 21, 1789; (HR1A-A1); (National Archives Microfilm Publication M1264, roll 1); Journals of the House of Representatives, 1789-1792; 1st Congress; Records of the U.S. House of Representatives, Record Group 233; National Archives Building, Washington, DC.

5. Enrolled original of the Bill of Rights, September 28, 1789; (National Archives Microfilm Publication M338, roll 1); Certificates of Ratification of the Constitution and the Bill of Rights, Including Related Correspondence and Rejections of Proposed Amendments, 1787-1792; General Records of the U.S. Government, Record Group 11; National Archives Building, Washington, DC.

6. Virginia Ratification of the Bill of Rights, December 15, 1791; (National Archives Microfilm Publication M338, roll 1); Certificates of Ratification of the Constitution and the Bill of Rights, Including Related Correspondence and Rejection of Proposed Amendments, 1787-1792; General Records of the U.S. Government, Record Group 11; National Archives Building, Washington, DC.

7. Fourteenth Amendment to the Constitution, June 16, 1886; Enrolled Acts Part III, 39th Congress; Enrolled Acts and Resolutions of Congress, 1789-1999; General Records of the U.S. Government, Record Group 11; National Archives at College Park, College Park, MD.

8. Petition for a writ of error in the Slaughterhouse cases, May 13, 1870; Case File 5599, pp. 103-105; Appellate Jurisdiction Records; Case Files, 1792-; Records of the Supreme Court of the United States, Record Group 267; National Archives Building, Washington, DC.

9. H.C. Whitley's report to Attorney General George Williams about the Ku Klux Klan, September 29, 1871; File 230/1/40/6, Box 47; Letters Received; Source Chronological Files, 1871-1884, Treasury; General Records of the Department of Justice, Record Group 60; National Archives at College Park, College Park, MD.

10. Petition for the enforcement of the 14th amendment, January 19, 1874; Committee on the Judiciary; Petitions and Memorials on Civil Rights Legislation; (HR 43A-H8.3); 43rd Congress, 1st Session; Records of the U.S. House of Representatives, Record Group 233; National Archives Building, Washington, DC.

11. Amicus curiae brief of the American Civil Liberties Union in *Everson v. Board of Education of Ewing Township, New Jersey*, November 14, 1946; Case File 52, *Everson v. Board of Education of Ewing Township, New Jersey*; O.T. 1946; Appellate Jurisdiction Records; Case Files 1792-; Records of the Supreme Court of the United States, Record Group 267; National Archives Building, Washington, DC.

12. Resolution submitted by Senator Powell condemning Grant's General Order No. 11, January 5, 1863; Records of Legislative Proceedings; Bill and Resolutions Originating in the Senate; (SEN37A-B6); 37th Congress, 1st Session; Records of the U.S. Senate, Record Group 46; National Archives Building, Washington, DC.

13. Mandate in *West Virginia v. Barnette*, June 14, 1943; Case File 591, *West Virginia Board of Education v. Barnette*, Appellate Jurisdiction Records; Case Files 1792-; October Term 1942; Records of the Supreme Court of the United States, Record Group 267; National Archives Building, Washington, DC.

14. Petition for restoration of Thomas Cooper's fine, February 24, 1824; Records of Legislative Proceedings; Bills and Resolutions Originating in the Senate; (SEN18A-D14); 18th Congress, 1st Session; Records of the U.S. Senate, Record Group 46; National Archives Building, Washington, DC.

15. The Espionage Act, June 15, 1917; Public Law 24, pp. 1, 17; (National Archives Microfilm Publication M1326, roll 52); Enrolled Acts and Resolutions of Congress, 1893-1956; General Records of the U.S. Government, Record Group 11; National Archives Building, Washington, DC.

16. "Garfield Wastes Coals and Electric Lights," *Los Angeles Daily Times*, November 12, 1917; File 9-12-153; Central Files; Classified Subject Files, Enclosures; General Records of the Department of Justice, Record Group 60; National Archives at College Park, College Park, MD.

17. John O'Brian's letter to U.S. Attorney Hooper Alexander about *The Finished Mystery*, May 15, 1918; File 9-19-1700-11-12, Central Files, Classified Subject Files, Correspondence; General Records of the Department of Justice, Record Group 60; National Archives at College Park, College Park, MD.

18. Poster, "True Blue," 1919; Case File B-584; Records Relating to the Espionage Act, World War I, 1917-1921; Records of the Post Office Department, Record Group 28; National Archives Building, Washington, DC.

19. Samuel Young's letter to the Clerk of the Supreme Court about *Gitlow v. New York*, November 6, 1925; Case File 29320, *Gitlow v. New York*; Appellate Jurisdiction Records; Case Files 1792-; Records of the Supreme Court of the United States, Record Group 267; National Archives Building, Washington, DC.

20. Testimony of John Tinker in *Tinker v. Des Moines*, July 25, 1966; Case File 21, *Tinker v. Des Moines*; Appellate Jurisdiction Records; Case Files 1792-; October Term 1968; Records of the Supreme Court of the United States, Record Group 267; National Archives Building, Washington, DC.

21. Smothers Brothers' letter to President Johnson, October 31, 1968; File Ex SP 3-274/Pro, Box 254; White House Central Files; Lyndon Baines Johnson Presidential Library, Austin, TX.

22. Lawrence Jones' Letter to Senator Warren Magnuson about federal firearms legislation, December 18, 1963; Records of Standing Committees; Committee on Commerce; Bill Files, S. 2345; (SEN88A-E6); 88th Congress, 1st Session; Records of the U.S. Senate, Record Group 46; National Archives Building, Washington, DC.

23. Answer to response to petition for a writ of certiorari in *Gideon v. Wainwright*, April 19, 1962; Case File #155, *Gideon v. Wainwright*; Appellate Jurisdiction Records; Case Files 1792-; October Term 1962; Records of the Supreme Court of the United States, Record Group 267; National Archives Building, Washington, DC.

24. Affidavit in forma pauperis from *Miranda v. Arizona*, July 13, 1965; Case File 759, File 2, *Miranda v. Arizona*; Appellate Jurisdiction Records; Case Records 1792-; October Term 1965; Records of the Supreme Court of the United States, Record Group 267; National Archives Building, Washington, DC.

25. Selections from the transcript of record of *Furman v. Georgia*, August 11, 1967, and September 20, 1968; Case File 69, *Furman v. Georgia*; Appellate Jurisdiction Records; Case Files 1792-; Records of the Supreme Court of the United States, Record Group 267; National Archives Building, Washington, DC.

26. *Legislative Notice* about S. (Senate Bill) 1765, February 1, 1984; Legislative Files, Subcommittee on Criminal Law; Senate Judiciary Committee; 98th Congress; Records of the U.S. Senate, Record Group 46; National Archives Building, Washington, DC.

27. House Joint Resolution 184, proposing an amendment to control child labor, December 3, 1923; (National Archives Microfilm Publication M1326, roll 63); Enrolled Acts and Resolutions of Congress, 1893-1956; General Records of the U.S. Government, Record Group 11; National Archives Building, Washington, DC.

28. Proclamation by President Eisenhower of Child Health Day, April 2, 1956; Presidential Proclamations; General Records of the U.S. Government, Record Group 11; National Archives at College Park, College Park, MD.

29. National Defense Education Act, September 2, 1958; Public Law 85-864; General Records of the U.S. Government, Record Group 11; National Archives Building, Washington, DC.

30. Commitment order to state industrial school from the case of *in re Gault*, June 15, 1964; Case File 116, *in re Gault*; Appellate Jurisdiction Records; Case Files 1792-; October Term 1965; Records of the Supreme Court of the United States, Record Group 267; National Archives Building, Washington, DC.

31. Ralph Evans' letter to Justice Douglas about *Goss v. Lopez*, 1974; Case File 73-898, Goss v. Lopez; Appellate Jurisdiction Records; Case File 1792-; Records of the Supreme Court of the United States, Record Group 267; National Archives Building, Washington, DC.

32. Executive Order No. 9066, February 19, 1942; Executive Orders, October 20, 1862-December 31, 1957; General Records of the U.S. Government, Record Group 11; National Archives Building, Washington, DC.

33. Public Law 503, March 21, 1942; (National Archives Microfilm Publication M1326, roll 103); Enrolled Acts and Resolutions of Congress, 1893-1956; General Records of the U.S. Government, Record Group 11; National Archives Building, Washington, DC.

34. Map, Relocation Project Sites, June 5, 1943; Volume 24, Final Report, Japanese Evacuation from the West Coast, 1942, Figure 21, pp. 256-257; Bound Volumes Concerning the Internment of Japanese-Americans, 1942-1945; Wartime Civil Control Administration; Western Defense Command and 4th Army; Records of the U.S. Army Commands, Record Group 338; National Archives Building, Washington, DC.

35. Judgement in *Korematsu v. United States*, December 18, 1944; Case File 22, *Korematsu v. United States*; Appellate Jurisdiction Records; Case Files 1792-; October Term 1944; Records of the Supreme Court of the United States, Record Group 267; National Archives Building, Washington DC.

36. Petition requesting reconsideration of Japanese-American evacuation, April 15, 1942; 014.31 Aliens, Volume II; Wartime Civil Control Administration General Correspondence 1942-1946 (Unclassified); Western Defense Command and 4th Army; Records of the U.S. Army Commands, Record Group 338; National Archives Building, Washington, DC.

37. Newspaper Column, "The Fifth Column On The Coast," by Walter Lippman, February 12, 1942; ASW 014.311; Formerly Security Classified Correspondence of John C. McCloy, 1941-1945; Records of the Office of the Secretary of War, Record Group 107; National Archives Building, Washington, DC.

38. Essay, "The Fence," by an evacuee, August 11, 1943; Document 26; File 61.3134 #3; (National Archives Microfilm Production M1342, roll 16); August-September 1943; Community Analysis Report, Heart Mountain; Field Basic Documentation, 1942-1946; Records of the War Relocation Authority, Record Group 210; National Archives Building, Washington, DC.

39. Chart, "Age, Sex, and Nativity Composition, Heart Mountain, Wyoming," November 1942; Heart Mountain, Quarterly Report, November 1942, p. 17; Field Basic Documentation, 1942-1946; Records of the War Relocation Authority, Record Group 210; National Archives Building, Washington, DC.

40. Watercolor of Heart Mountain by Estelle Ishigo, February 10, 1943; Heart Mountain, Quarterly Report, February 1943, pp. 71-72; Field Basic Documentation, 1942-1946; Records of the War Relocation Authority, Record Group 210; National Archives Building, Washington, DC.

41. Photograph No. NWDNS-210-G-E98; "Heart Mountain," November 1942; Records of the War Relocation Board, Record Group 210; National Archives at College Park, College Park, MD.

42. Church Journal, *Heart Mountain Buddhist's Digest*, July 7, 1943; Document 40; File 61.314 #5; Heart Mountain; Community Analysis Reports; Headquarters Subject-Classified General Files; Records of the War Relocation Authority, Record Group 210; National Archives Building, Washington, DC.

43. Yearbook, Hunt High School *Memoirs*, 1944; Minidoka; Yearbooks; Field Basic Documentation, 1942-1946; Records of the War Relocation Authority, Record Group 210; National Archives Building, Washington, DC.

44. Interview with the Student Relocation Counselor of Topaz, UT, April 1944; Document 30; File 61.310.2; Central Utah; Community Analysis Reports; Headquarters Subject-Classified General Files; Records of the War Relocation Authority, Record Group 210; National Archives Building, Washington, DC.

45. Advertisement, "Heed Their Rising Voices," March 29, 1960; Case File 39, File 2; Appellate Jurisdiction Records; Case Files 1792-; October Term 1963; Records of the Supreme Court of the United States, Record Group 267; National Archives Building, Washington, DC.

46. S. 1160, which became the Freedom of Information Act, October 4, 1965; Committee on the Judiciary; Records of the Committees; (SEN89A-E12); 89th Congress; Bill Files; Records of the U.S. Senate, Record Group 46; National Archives Building, Washington, DC.

18th **CONGRESS**,
2d Session.

[38]

IN SENATE OF THE UNITED STATES.

February 24, 1825.

Mr. Dickerson, from the Select Committee to whom was referred the petition of Thomas Cooper, President of the South Carolina College,

REPORTED:

That the petitioner states, that, in the month of April, 1800, at the city of Philadelphia, he was indicted and found guilty of having printed and published what was alleged to be a libel against Mr. John Adams, the then President of the United States, under the act commonly called the sedition law, passed the 14th of July, 1798; the second section whereof runs as follows, viz:—" *And be it further enacted,* That if any person shall write, print, utter, or publish, or shall cause or procure to be written, printed, uttered, or published, or shall, knowingly or willingly, assist or aid in writing, printing, uttering, or publishing, any false, scandalous, and malicious writing or writings, against the Government of the United States, or either House of Congress of the United States, or the President of the United States, with an intent to defame the Government of the United States, or either House of the said Congress, or the President, or to bring them, or either of them, into contempt or disrepute, or to excite against them, or either, or any, of them, the hatred of the good people of the United States, &c. then such person being thereof convicted, before any court of the United States having jurisdiction thereof, shall be punished by fine, not exceeding two thousand dollars, and by imprisonment not exceeding two years." He further states, that, under this section, he was sentenced, upon a conviction of having printed and published the above alleged libel, to pay a fine of four hundred dollars, and to be imprisoned during six months. He further states, that, on the day when his imprisonment expired, he paid into the hands of John Hall, Esq. Marshal for the District of Pennsylvania, the aforesaid fine of four hundred dollars, for the use of the Treasury of the United States. He further states, that the law under which he was convicted, called the sedition law, was an unconstitutional law, such as the legislature that passed it had no right to enact; and that the fine so exacted from and paid by him, was illegally exacted and ought not to be retained. He therefore prays, that the fine so paid by him may be restored, with interest.

About the National Archives: A Word to Educators

The National Archives and Records Administration (NARA) is responsible for the preservation and use of the permanently valuable records of the federal government. These materials provide evidence of the activities of the government from 1774 to the present in the form of written and printed documents, maps and posters, sound recordings, photographs, films, computer tapes, and other media. These rich archival sources are useful to everyone: federal officials seeking information on past government activities, citizens needing data for use in legal matters, historians, social scientists and public policy planners, environmentalists, historic preservationists, medical researchers, architects and engineers, novelists and playwrights, journalists researching stories, students preparing papers, and persons tracing their ancestry or satisfying their curiosity about particular historical events. These records are useful to you as educators either in preparing your own instructional materials or pursuing your own research.

The National Archives records are organized by the governmental body that created them rather than under a library's subject/author/title categories. There is no Dewey decimal or Library of Congress designation; each departmental bureau or collection of agency's records is assigned a record group number. In lieu of a card catalog, inventories and other finding aids assist the researcher in locating material in records not originally created for research purposes, often consisting of thousands of cubic feet of documentation.

The National Archives is a public institution whose records and research facilities nationwide are open to anyone 14 years of age and over. These facilities are found in the Washington, DC, metropolitan area, in the 11 Presidential libraries, the Nixon Presidential Materials Project, and in 16 regional archives across the nation. Whether you are pursuing broad historical questions or are interested in the history of your family, admittance to the research room at each location requires only that you fill out a simple form stating your name, address, and research interest. A staff member then issues an identification card, which is good for two years.

If you come to do research, you will be offered an initial interview with a reference archivist. You will also be able to talk with archivists who have custody of the records. If you have a clear definition of your questions and have prepared in advance by reading as many of the secondary sources as possible, you will find that these interviews can be very helpful in guiding you to the research material you need.

The best printed source of information about the overall holdings of the National Archives is the *Guide to the National Archives of the United States* (issued in 1974, reprinted in 1988), which is available in university libraries and many public libraries and online at **www.nara.gov**. The *Guide* describes in very general terms the records in the National Archives, gives the background and history of each agency represented by those records, and provides useful information about access to the records. To accommodate users outside of Washington, DC, the regional archives hold microfilm copies of much that is found in Washington. In addition, the regional archives contain records created by field offices of the federal government, including district and federal appellate court records, records of the Bureau of Indian Affairs, National Park Service, Bureau of Land Management, Forest Service, Bureau of the Census, and others. These records are particularly useful for local and regional history studies and in linking local with national historical events.

For more information about the National Archives and its educational and cultural programs, visit NARA's Web site at **www.nara.gov**.

Presidential Libraries

Herbert Hoover Library
210 Parkside Drive
West Branch, IA 52358-0488
319-643-5301

Franklin D. Roosevelt Library
511 Albany Post Road
Hyde Park, NY 12538-1999
914-229-8114

Harry S. Truman Library
500 West U.S. Highway 24
Independence, MO 64050-1798
816-833-1400

Dwight D. Eisenhower Library
200 Southeast Fourth Street
Abilene, KS 67410-2900
785-263-4751

John Fitzgerald Kennedy Library
Columbia Point
Boston, MA 02125-3398
617-929-4500

Lyndon Baines Johnson Library
2313 Red River Street
Austin, TX 78705-5702
512-916-5137

Gerald R. Ford Library
1000 Beal Avenue
Ann Arbor, MI 48109-2114
734-741-2218

Jimmy Carter Library
441 Freedom Parkway
Atlanta, GA 30307-1498
404-331-3942

Ronald Reagan Library
40 Presidential Drive
Simi Valley, CA 93065-0600
805-522-8444/800-410-8354

George Bush Library
1000 George Bush Drive
P.O. Box 10410
College Station, TX 77842-0410
409-260-9552

Clinton Presidential Materials Project
1000 LaHarpe Boulevard
Little Rock, AR 72201
501-254-6866

National Archives Regional Archives

NARA-Northeast Region
380 Trapelo Road
Waltham, MA 02452-6399
781-647-8104

NARA-Northeast Region
10 Conte Drive
Pittsfield, MA 01201-8230
413-445-6885

NARA-Northeast Region
201 Varick Street, 12th Floor
New York, NY 10014-4811
212-337-1300

NARA-Mid Atlantic Region
900 Market Street
Philadelphia, PA 19107-4292
215-597-3000

NARA-Mid Atlantic Region
14700 Townsend Road
Philadelphia, PA 19154-1096
215-671-9027

NARA-Southeast Region
1557 St. Joseph Avenue
East Point, GA 30344-2593
404-763-7474

NARA-Great Lakes Region
7358 South Pulaski Road
Chicago, IL 60629-5898
773-581-7816

NARA-Great Lakes Region
3150 Springboro Road
Dayton, OH 45439-1883
937-225-2852

NARA-Central Plains Region
2312 East Bannister Road
Kansas City, MO 64131-3011
816-926-6272

NARA-Central Plains Region
200 Space Center Drive
Lee's Summit, MO 64064-1182
816-478-7079

NARA-Southwest Region
501 West Felix Street
P.O. Box 6216
Fort Worth, TX 76115-0216
817-334-5525

NARA-Rocky Mountain Region
Denver Federal Center, Building 48
P.O. Box 25307
Denver, CO 80225-0307
303-236-0804

NARA-Pacific Region
24000 Avila Road
P.O. Box 6719
Laguna Niguel, CA 92607-6719
949-360-2641

NARA-Pacific Region
1000 Commodore Drive
San Bruno, CA 94066-2350
650-876-9009

NARA-Pacific Alaska Region
6125 Sand Point Way, NE
Seattle, WA 98115-7999
206-526-6507

NARA-Pacific Alaska Region
654 West Third Avenue
Anchorage, AK 99501-2145
907-271-2443

Reproductions of Documents

Reproductions of the oversized print documents included in these units are available in their original size by special order from Graphic Visions.

dissolved contrary to the rights of the people, when they attempted to deliberate on grievances; and their dutiful, humble, loyal & reasonable petitions to the crown for redress have been repeatedly treated with contempt by his majesty's ministers of state.

The good people of the several colonies of Newhampshire, Massachusets-bay, Rhode island and Providence plantations, Connecticut, Newyork, New-Jersey, Pensylvania, New castle Kent and Sussex on Delaware, Maryland, Virginia, North Carolina and South-Carolina justly alarmed at these arbitrary proceedings of parliament and administration have severally elected, constituted and appointed deputies to meet and sit in general congress in the city of Philadelphia in order to obtain such establishment as that their religion, laws and liberties may not be subverted:

Whereupon the deputies so appointed being now assembled in a full and free representation of these colonies, taking into their most serious consideration, the best means of attaining the ends aforesaid do in the first place as Englishmen their ancestors in like cases have usually done, for asserting and vindicating their rights and liberties Declare—

That the inhabitants of the English colonies in North America by the immutable laws of Nature, the principles of the English constitution, and the several charters or compacts have the following Rights—

1. Resolved N.C.D.1. That they are entitled to life, liberty & property: and they have never ceded to any sovereign power whatever a right to dispose of either without their consent.

Resolved N.C.D. 2. That our ancestors, who first settled these colonies were, at the time of their emigration from the mother country, entitled to all the rights, liberties and immunities of free and natural born subjects, within the realm of England.

Resolved

Resolved. N.C.D. 3. That by such emigration, they by no means forfeited, surrendered or lost any of those rights, but that they were, and their descendants now are entitled to the exercise and enjoyment of all such of them, as their local and other circumstances enable them to exercise and enjoy.

Resolved. 4. That the foundation of english liberty and of all free government is a right in the people, to participate in their legislative council: and as the English colonists are not represented, and from their local and other circumstances cannot be properly represented in the British parliament, they are entitled to a free and exclusive power of legislation in their several provincial legislatures, where their right of representation can alone be preserved, in all cases of taxation and internal polity, subject only to the negative of their sovereign, in such manner, as has been heretofore used and accustomed: But, from the necessity of the case, and a regard to the mutual interests of both countries we cheerfully consent to the operation of such acts of the British parliament, as are bona fide, restrained to the regulation of our external commerce, for the purpose of securing the commercial advantages of the whole empire to the mother country, and the commercial benefits of its respective members, excluding every idea of taxation internal or external for raising a revenue on the subjects in America without their consent.

Resolved N.C.D. 5. That the respective colonies are entitled to the common law of England, and more especially to the great and inestimable priviledge of being tried by their peers of the vicinage according to the course of that law.

Resolved.

Document 1b. Declaration of Rights, October 14, 1774. [National Archives]

Resolved 6. That these ~~in every of these colonies~~ are entitled to the benefit of such of the English statutes, as existed at the time of their colonization, and which they have by experience respectively found to be applicable to their several local and other circumstances.

Resolved N.C.D 7. That these his majesty's colonies are likewise entitled to all the immunities and priviledges granted & confirmed to them by royal charters or secured by their several codes of provincial laws. —

Resolved N.C.D 8. That they have a right peaceably to assemble, consider of their grievances and petition the king; and that all prosecutions, prohibitory proclamations and commitments for the same are illegal.

Resolved N.C.D. 9. That the keeping a standing army in these colonies in times of peace, without the consent of the legislature of that colony, in which such army is kept is against law. —

Resolved N.C.D. 10. It is indispensibly necessary to good government and rendered essential by the English constitution, that the constituent branches of the legislature be independant of each other: that therefore the exercise of legislative power in several colonies by a council appointed during pleasure by the crown is uncon-stitutional, ~~dangerous~~ and destructive to the freedom of American legislation.

All and each of which, the aforesaid deputies in behalf of themselves and their constituents do claim demand and insist on as their indubitable rights and liberties, which cannot be legally taken from

State of Rhode Island

At a Town Meeting of the Freemen of the Town of Providence, holden by Adjournment at the State House in Providence, on the 3d Day of July 1779 ~

Whereas many of the Inhabitants of this Town, have been at great Expence and have suffered much on account of the Troops having been Barracked upon the Inhabitants Since the Enemy have been in Possesion of Rhode Island: and As the whole Community of the United States are Equally concerned in and benefited by the War and as far as may be ought Equally to Bear and Support the Burthen thereof. and it is Right and Just that the Expence of Providing Barracks for the Troops should be defreyed and borne by the Public in General:

It is therefore VOTED and RESOLVED That Nicholas Brown Esqr Ephraim Bowen Esqr and James Mitchel Varnum Esqr be and they hereby are appointed a Committee to draft a Letter on this Subject to the Delegates in Congress from this State, representing the Situation of the Town and requesting them to Use their Endeavours that Barracks be provided at the Expence of the United States for the Accommodation of the Troops in Case it shall be necessary that any be Quartered in this Town the ensuing Winter ~

A True Copy

Attest. Theodore Foster Town Clerk

Document 2. Resolution of Providence, RI, to ask Congress for money to quarter troops, July 3, 1779. [National Archives]

State of North-Carolina.
IN CONVENTION, AUGUST 1, 1788.

Resolved, That a Declaration of Rights, asserting and securing from incroachment the great Principles of civil and religious Liberty, and the unalienable Rights of the People, together with Amendments to the most ambiguous and exceptionable Parts of the said Constitution of Government, ought to be laid before Congress, and the Convention of the States that shall or may be called for the Purpose of Amending the said Constitution, for their consideration, previous to the Ratification of the Constitution aforesaid, on the part of the State of North Carolina.

DECLARATION OF RIGHTS

1st. That there are certain natural rights of which men, when they form a social compact, cannot deprive or divest their posterity, among which are the enjoyment of life, and liberty, with the means of acquiring, possessing and protecting property, and pursuing and obtaining happiness and safety.

2d. That all power is naturally vested in, and consequently derived from the people; that magistrates therefore are their trustees, and agents, and at all times amenable to them.

3d. That Government ought to be instituted for the common benefit, protection and security of the people; and that the doctrine of non-resistance against arbitrary power and oppression is absurd, slavish, and destructive to the good and happiness of mankind.

4th. That no man or set of men are entitled to exclusive or separate public emoluments or privileges from the community, but in consideration of public services; which not being descendible, neither ought the offices of magistrate, legislator or judge, or any other public office to be hereditary.

5th. That the legislative, executive and judiciary powers of government should be separate and distinct, and that the members of the two first may be restrained from oppression by feeling and participating the public burthens, they should at fixed periods be reduced to a private station, return into the mass of the people; and the vacancies be supplied by certain and regular elections; in which all or any part of the former members to be eligible or ineligible, as the rules of the Constitution of Government, and the laws shall direct.

6th. That elections of Representatives in the legislature ought to be free and frequent, and all men having sufficient evidence of permanent common interest with, and attachment to the community, ought to have the right of suffrage: and no aid, charge, tax or fee can be set, rated, or levied upon the people without their own consent, or that of their representatives, so elected, nor can they be bound by any law, to which they have not in like manner assented for the public good.

7th. That all power of suspending laws, or the execution of laws by any authority without the consent of the representatives, of the people in the Legislature, is injurious to their rights, and ought not to be exercised.

8th. That in all capital and criminal prosecutions, a man hath a right to demand the cause and nature of his accusation, to be confronted with the accusers and witnesses, to call for evidence and be allowed counsel in his favor, and to a fair and speedy trial by an impartial jury of his vicinage, without whose unanimous consent he cannot be found guilty (except in the government of the land and naval forces) nor can he be compelled to give evidence against himself.

9th. That no freeman ought to be taken, imprisoned, or disseized of his freehold, liberties, privileges or franchises, or outlawed or exiled, or in any manner destroyed or deprived of his life, liberty, or property but by the law of the land.

10th. That every freeman restrained of his liberty is entitled to a remedy to enquire into the lawfulness thereof, and to remove the same, if unlawful, and that such remedy ought not to be denied nor delayed.

11th. That in controversies respecting property, and in suits between man and man, the ancient trial by jury is one of the greatest securities to the rights of the people, and ought to remain sacred and inviolable.

12th. That every freeman ought to find a certain remedy by recourse to the laws for all injuries and wrongs he may receive in his person, property, or character. He ought to obtain right and justice freely without sale, completely and without denial, promptly and without delay, and that all establishments, or regulations contravening these rights, are oppressive and unjust.

13th. That excessive bail ought not to be required, nor excessive fines imposed, nor cruel and unusual punishments inflicted.

14. That every freeman has a right to be secure from all unreasonable searches, and seizures of his person, his papers, and property: all warrants therefore to search suspected places, or seize any freeman, his papers or property, without information upon oath (or affirmation of a person religiously scrupulous of taking an oath) of legal and sufficient cause, are grievous and oppressive, and all general warrants to search suspected places, or to apprehend any suspected person without specially naming or describing the place or person, are dangerous and ought not to be granted.

15th. That the people have a right peaceably to assemble together to consult for the common good, or to instruct their representatives; and that every freeman has a right to petition or apply to the Legislature for redress of grievances.

16th. That the people have a right to freedom of speech, and of writing and publishing their sentiments; that the freedom of the press is one of the greatest bulwarks of Liberty, and ought not to be violated.

17th. That the people have a right to keep and bear arms; that a well regulated militia composed of the body of the people, trained to arms, is the proper, natural and safe defence of a free state. That standing armies in time of peace are dangerous to Liberty, and therefore ought to be avoided, as far as the circumstances and protection of the community will admit; and that in all cases, the military should be under strict subordination to, and governed by the civil power.

18th. That no soldier in time of peace ought to be quartered in any house without the consent of the owner, and in time of war in such manner only as the Laws direct.

19th. That any person religiously scrupulous of bearing arms ought to be exempted upon payment of an equivalent to employ another to bears arms in his stead.

20. That religion, or the duty which we owe to our Creator, and the manner of discharging it, can be directed only by reason and conviction, not by force or violence, and therefore all men have an equal, natural and unalienable right to the free exercise of religion according to the dictates of conscience, and that no particular religious sect or society ought to be favoured or established by law in preference to others.

Amendments to the Constitution.

I. THAT each state in the union shall, respectively, retain every power, jurisdiction and right, which is not by this constitution delegated to the Congress of the United States, or to the departments of the Federal Government.

II. That there shall be one representative for every 30,000, according to the enumeration or census, mentioned in the constitution, until the whole number of representatives amounts to two hundred; after which, that number shall be continued or increased, as Congress shall direct, upon the principles fixed in the constitution, by apportioning the representatives of each state to some greater number of people from time to time, as population encreases.

III. When Congress shall lay direct taxes or excises, they shall immediately inform the executive power of each state, of the quota of such state, according to the census herein directed, which is proposed to be thereby raised: And if the legislature of any state shall pass a law, which shall be effectual for raising such quota at the time required by Congress, the taxes and excises laid by Congress shall not be collected in such state.

IV. That the members of the senate and house of representatives shall be ineligible to, and incapable of holding any civil office under the authority of the United States, during the time for which they shall, respectively, be elected.

V. That the journals of the proceedings of the senate and house of representatives shall be published at least once in every year, except such parts thereof relating to treaties, alliances, or military operations, as in their judgment require secrecy.

VI. That a regular statement and account of the receipts and expenditures of the public money shall be published at least once in every year.

VII. That no commercial treaty shall be ratified without the concurrence of two-thirds of the whole number of the members of the senate: And no treaty, ceding, contracting, or restraining or suspending the territorial rights or claims of the United States, or any of them or their, or any of their rights or claims to fishing in the American seas, or navigating the American rivers shall be made, but in cases of the most urgent and extreme necessity; nor shall any such treaty be ratified without the concurrence of three-fourths of the whole number of the members of both houses respectively.

VIII. That no navigation law, or law regulating commerce shall be passed without the consent of two-thirds of the members present in both houses.

IX. That no standing army or regular troops shall be raised or kept up in time of peace, without the consent of two thirds of the members present in both houses.

X. That no soldier shall be inlisted for any longer term than four years, except in time of war, and then for no longer term than the continuance of the war.

XI. That each state, respectively, shall have the power to provide for organizing, arming and disciplining its own militia whensoever Congress shall omit or neglect to provide for the same. That the militia shall not be subject to martial law, except when in actual service in time of war, invasion or rebellion: And when not in the actual service of the United States, shall be subject only to such fines, penalties, and punishments as shall be directed or inflicted by the laws of its own state.

XII. That Congress shall not declare any state, to be in rebellion without the consent of at least two-thirds of all the members present of both houses.

XIII. That the exclusive power of Legislation given to Congress over the federal town and its adjacent district, and other places, purchased or to be purchased by Congress, of any of the states, shall extend only to such regulations as respect the police and good government thereof.

XIV. That no person shall be capable of being president of the United States for more than eight years in any term of sixteen years.

XV. That the judicial power of the United States shall be vested in one supreme court, and in such courts of admiralty as Congress may from time to time ordain and establish in any of the different states. The judicial power shall extend to all cases in law and equity, arising under treaties made, or which shall be made under the authority of the United States; to all cases affecting ambassadors, other foreign ministers and consuls; to all cases of admiralty, and maritime jurisdiction; to controversies to which the United States shall be a party; to controversies between two or more states, and between parties claiming lands under the grants of different states. In all cases affecting ambassadors, other foreign ministers and consuls, and those in which a state shall be a party, the supreme court shall have original jurisdiction, in all other cases before mentioned; the supreme court shall have appellate jurisdiction as to matters of law only, except in cases of equity, and of admiralty and maritime jurisdiction, in which the supreme court shall have appellate jurisdiction both as to law and fact, with such exceptions, and under such regulations as the Congress shall make. But the judicial power of the United States shall extend to no case where the cause of action shall have originated before the ratification of this constitution, except in disputes between states about their territory; disputes between persons claiming lands under the grants of different states, and suits for debts due to the united states.

XVI. That in criminal prosecutions, no man shall be restrained in the exercise of the usual and accustomed right of challenging or excepting to the jury.

XVII. That Congress shall not alter, modify, or interfere in the times, places, or manner of holding elections for senators and representatives, or either of them, except when the legislature of any state shall neglect, refuse or be disabled by invasion or rebellion, to prescribe the same.

XVIII. That those clauses which declare that Congress shall not exercise certain powers, be not interpreted in any manner whatsoever to extend the powers of Congress; but that they be construed either as making exceptions to the specified powers where this shall be the case, or otherwise, as inserted merely for greater caution.

XIX. That the laws ascertaining the compensation of senators and representatives for their services be postponed in their operation, until after the election of representatives immediately succeeding the passing thereof, that excepted, which shall first be passed on the subject.

XX. That some tribunal, other than the senate, be provided for trying impeachments of senators.

XXI. That the salary of a judge shall not be increased or diminished during his continuance in office, otherwise than by general regulations of salary which may take place, on a revision of the subject at stated periods of not less than seven years, to commence from the time such salaries shall be first ascertained by Congress.

XXII. That Congress erect no company of merchants with exclusive advantages of commerce.

XXIII. That no treaties which shall be directly opposed to the existing laws of the United States in Congress assembled, shall be valid until such laws shall be repealed, or made conformable to such treaty; nor shall any treaty be valid which is contradictory to the constitution of the United States.

XXIV. That the latter part of the fifth paragraph of the 9th section of the first article be altered to read thus,—Nor shall vessels bound to a particular state be obliged to enter or pay duties in any other; nor when bound from any one of the States be obliged to clear in another.

XXV. That Congress shall not directly or indirectly, either by themselves or thro' the judiciary, interfere with any one of the states in the redemption of paper money already emitted and now in circulation, or in liquidating and discharging the public securities of any one of the states: But each and every state shall have the exclusive right of making such laws and regulations for the above purposes as they shall think proper.

XXVI. That Congress shall not introduce foreign troops into the United States without the consent of two-thirds of the members present of both houses.

By order J Hunt, Secretary

Sam'l Johnston, President

appointment of Commissioners for managing the same", for his approbation.

A message was received from the President of the United States, notifying that the President approves of the Act, intituled "An Act providing for the expences which "may attend negociations or treaties with the Indian tribes, and the appointment of "Commissioners for managing the same", and has this day affixed his signature thereto: And the messenger delivered in the said Act, and then withdrew.

The Order of the day for the House to resolve itself into a Committee of the whole House on the Bill sent from the Senate, intituled "An Act to establish "the Judicial Courts of the United States"; also on the Bill for establishing a Land Office in, and for the Western territory, and on the Bill to provide for the safe keeping of the Acts, Records, and Seal of the United States; for the due publication of the Acts of Congress; for the authentication of the copies of Records; for making out, and recording Commissions and prescribing their form, and for establishing the fees of Office to be taken for making such Commissions, and for copies of Records and papers, were read, and postponed until tomorrow.

And then the House adjourned until tomorrow morning, eleven o'clock.

Friday, the 21st of August.

The House resumed the consideration of the amendments made by the Committee of the whole House to the report from the Committee of eleven, to whom it was referred to take the subject of Amendments to the Constitution of the United States, generally into their consideration; and the said Amendments being partly agreed to, and partly disagreed to:

The House proceeded to consider the original report of the Committee of eleven, consisting of seventeen Articles, as now amended; Whereupon, the first, second, third, fourth, fifth, sixth, seventh, eighth, ninth, tenth, eleventh, twelfth, tenth, fourteenth, fifteenth, and sixteenth Articles, being again read, and debated

Document 4a. House journal recording the 17 amendments proposed for a bill of rights, August 21, 1789. [National Archives]

debated, were, upon the question severally put thereupon, agreed to by the House, as follow, (two thirds of the Members present concurring,) to wit:

I. After the first enumeration, there shall be one representative for every thirty thousand until the number shall amount to one hundred, after which the proportion shall be so regulated by Congress, that there shall be not less than one hundred Representatives, nor less than one representative for every forty thousand persons, until the number of Representatives shall amount to two hundred: after which the proportion shall be so regulated, that there shall not be less than two hundred representatives, nor less than one representative for every fifty thousand persons.

II. No law varying the compensation to the Members of Congress shall take effect until an election of Representatives shall have intervened.

III. Congress shall make no law establishing religion, or prohibiting the free exercise thereof, nor shall the rights of conscience be infringed.

IV. That the freedom of Speech, and of the press, and the right of the people peaceably to assemble and consult for their common good, and to apply to the government for redress of grievances, shall not be infringed.

V. A well regulated Militia composed of the body of the people, being the best security of a free State, the right of the people to keep, and bear Arms, shall not be infringed; but no one religiously scrupulous of bearing Arms, shall be compelled to render military service in person.

VI. No soldier shall in time of peace be quartered in any house, without the consent of the owner, nor in time of war, but in a manner to be prescribed by law.

VII. No person shall be subject, except in case of impeachment, to more than one trial, or one punishment for the same Offence, nor shall be compelled, in any criminal case, to be a witness against himself, nor be deprived of life, liberty, or property, without due process of law; nor shall private property be taken for public use, without just compensation.

VIII. Excessive bail shall not be required, nor excessive fines imposed, nor cruel and unusual punishments inflicted.

Document 4b. House journal recording the 17 amendments proposed for a bill of rights, August 21, 1789. [National Archives]

IX. The right of the people to be secure in their persons, houses, papers, and effects against unreasonable searches and seizures, shall not be violated: and no Warrants shall issue, but upon probable cause, supported by oath or affirmation, and particularly describing the place to be searched, and the persons or things to be seized.

X. The enumeration in this Constitution of certain rights shall not be construed to deny, or disparage others retained by the people.

XI. No State shall infringe the right of trial by jury in criminal cases, nor the rights of conscience, nor the freedom of speech, or of the press.

XII. No appeal to the Supreme Court of the United States shall be allowed, where the value in controversy shall not amount to one thousand dollars; nor shall any fact, triable by a jury, according to the course of the common law, be otherwise re-examinable than according to the rules of Common law.

XIII. In all criminal prosecutions, the accused shall enjoy the right to a speedy and public trial, to be informed of the nature and cause of the accusation, to be confronted with the witnesses against him, to have compulsory process for obtaining Witnesses in his favour, and to have the assistance of counsel for his defence.

XIV. The trial of all crimes, (except in cases of impeachment, and in cases arising in the land or naval forces, or in the militia, when in actual service, in time of war or public danger) shall be by an impartial jury of the vicinage, with the requisite of unanimity for conviction, the right of challenge, and other accustomed requisites: And no person shall be held to answer for a capital, or otherwise infamous crime, unless on a presentment or indictment by a Grand jury: but if a crime be committed in a place in the possession of an enemy, or in which an insurrection may prevail, the indictment and trial may by law be authorized in some other place within the same State.

XV. In suits at common law, the right of trial by jury shall be preserved.

XVI. The powers delegated by the Constitution to the government of the United

Document 4c. House journal recording the 17 amendments proposed for a bill of rights, August 21, 1789. [National Archives]

States, shall be conceived as therein appropriated, so that the Legislature shall not exercise the powers vested in the Executive or Judicial; nor the Executive the powers vested in the Legislature or Judicial; nor the Judicial the powers vested in the Legislative or Executive.

The Seventeenth Article in the words following, to wit: "The powers not delegated "by the Constitution, nor prohibited by it to the States, and reserved to the States "respectively", being under debate; a motion was made, and the question being put to amend the same, by inserting after the word "not", the word "expressly":

It passed in the negative, Ayes seventeen, Noes thirty two.

The Ayes and Noes being demanded by one fifth of the members present.

Those who voted in the affirmative are Edanus Burke, Isaac Coles, William Floyd, Elbridge Gerry, Jonathan Grout, John Hathorn, James Jackson, Samuel Livermore, John Page, Josiah Parker, George Partridge, Jeremiah Van Renselaer, William Smith (of South Carolina) Michael Jenifer Stone, Thomas Sumpter, George Thatcher, and Thomas Tudor Tucker.

Those who voted in the negative are, Fisher Ames, Egbert Benson, Elias Boudinot, John Brown, Lambert Cadwalader, Daniel Carroll, George Clymer, Thomas Fitzsimons, Abiel Foster, George Gale, Nicholas Gilman, Benjamin Goodhue, Thomas Hartley, Daniel Heister, John Laurance, Richard Bland Lee, James Madison junior, Andrew Moore, Peter Muhlenberg, James Schureman, Thomas Scott, Theodore Sedgwick, Joshua Seney, Roger Sherman, Peter Silvester, Thomas Sinnickson, William Smith (of Maryland) Jonathan Sturges, Jonathan Trumbull, John Vining, Jeremiah Wadsworth, and Henry Wynkoop.

And then the main question being put, that the House do agree to the saide seventeenth Article,

It was resolved in the affirmative, two thirds of the members present concurring,

a

Document 4d. House journal recording the 17 amendments proposed for a bill of rights, August 21, 1789. [National Archives]

A motion was then made and seconded to add to the said Articles, the following:

"Congress shall not alter, modify, or interfere in the times, places, or manner of "holding elections of Senators or Representatives, except when any State shall refuse "or neglect, or be unable by invasion or rebellion to make such election."

And on the question that the House do agree to the said proposed Articles

It passed in the negative. Ayes, twenty three; Noes twenty eight.

The Ayes and Noes being demanded by one fifth of the members present:

Those who voted in the affirmative are Ædanus Burke, Isaac Coles, William Floyd, Elbridge Gerry, Samuel Griffin, Jonathan Grout, John Hathorn, Daniel Heister, James Jackson, Samuel Livermore, George Mathews, Andrew Moore, John Page, Josiah Parker, George Partridge, Jeremiah Van Rensselaer, Joshua Seney, Peter Silvester, William Smith (of South Carolina) Michael Jenifer Stone, Thomas Sumpter, George Thatcher, and Thomas Tudor Tucker.

Those who voted in the negative are, Fisher Ames, Egbert Benson, Elias Boudinot, John Brown, Lambert Cadwalader, Daniel Carroll, George Clymer, Thomas Fitzsimons, Abiel Foster, George Gale, Nicholas Gilman, Benjamin Goodhue, Thomas Hartley, John Laurance, Richard Bland Lee, James Madison junior, Peter Muhlenberg, James Schureman, Thomas Scott, Theodore Sedgwick, Roger Sherman, Thomas Sinnickson, William Smith (of Maryland) Jonathan Sturges, Jonathan Trumbull, John Vining, Jeremiah Wadsworth, and Henry Wynkoop.

On motion, Ordered that the further consideration of Amendments to the Constitution of the United States, be postponed until to morrow.

The Orders of the day, for the House to resolve itself into a Committee of the whole House on the Bill sent from the Senate, intituled "An Act to establish "the Judicial Courts of the United States"; also, on the Bill for establishing a

171

a Land Office in, and for the Western territory; and on the Bill to provide for the safe keeping of the Acts, Records, and Seal of the United States; for the due publication of the Acts of Congress: for the Authentication of the copies of Records; for making out, and recording Commissions, and prescribing their form, and for establishing the fees of Office to be taken for making such Commissions, and for copies of Records and papers, were read, and postponed until to morrow.

And then the House adjourned until to morrow morning, eleven O'Clock.

Document 4f. House journal recording the 17 amendments proposed
for a bill of rights, August 21, 1789. [National Archives]

Congress OF THE United States

begun and held at the City of New-York, on
Wednesday the fourth of March, one thousand and seven hundred and eighty nine.

THE Conventions of a number of the States, having at the time of their adopting the Constitution, expressed a desire, in order to prevent misconstruction or abuse of its powers, that further declaratory and restrictive clauses should be added: And as extending the ground of public confidence in the Government, will best ensure the beneficent ends of its institution.

RESOLVED by the Senate and House of Representatives of the United States of America, in Congress assembled, two thirds of both Houses concurring, that the following Articles be proposed to the Legislatures of the several States, as amendments to the Constitution of the United States, all, or any of which Articles, when ratified by three fourths of the said Legislatures, to be valid to all intents and purposes, as part of the said Constitution, viz.

ARTICLES in addition to, and Amendment of the Constitution of the United States of America, proposed by Congress, and ratified by the Legislatures of the several States, pursuant to the fifth Article of the original Constitution.

Article the first.... After the first enumeration required by the first Article of the Constitution, there shall be one Representative for every thirty thousand, until the number shall amount to one hundred, after which, the proportion shall be so regulated by Congress, that there shall be not less than one hundred Representatives, nor less than one Representative for every forty thousand persons, until the number of Representatives shall amount to two hundred, after which the proportion shall be so regulated by Congress, that there shall not be less than two hundred Representatives, nor more than one Representative for every fifty thousand persons.

Article the second.... No law, varying the compensation for the services of the Senators and Representatives, shall take effect, until an election of Representatives shall have intervened.

Article the third... Congress shall make no law respecting an establishment of religion, or prohibiting the free exercise thereof; or abridging the freedom of speech, or of the press, or the right of the people peaceably to assemble, and to petition the Government for a redress of grievances.

Article the fourth.... A well regulated militia, being necessary to the security of a free State, the right of the people to keep and bear Arms, shall not be infringed.

Article the fifth....... No Soldier shall, in time of peace be quartered in any house, without the consent of the Owner, nor in time of war, but in a manner to be prescribed by law.

Article the sixth...... The right of the people to be secure in their persons, houses, papers, and effects, against unreasonable searches and seizures, shall not be violated, and no Warrants shall issue, but upon probable cause, supported by oath or affirmation, and particularly describing the place to be searched, and the persons or things to be seized.

Article the seventh... No person shall be held to answer for a capital, or otherwise infamous crime, unless on a presentment or indictment of a Grand Jury, except in cases arising in the land or naval forces, or in the Militia, when in actual service in time of War or public danger; nor shall any person be subject for the same offence to be twice put in jeopardy of life or limb, nor shall be compelled in any criminal case to be a witness against himself, nor be deprived of life, liberty, or property, without due process of law; nor shall private property be taken for public use, without just compensation.

Article the eighth... In all criminal prosecutions, the accused shall enjoy the right to a speedy and public trial, by an impartial jury of the State and district wherein the crime shall have been committed, which district shall have been previously ascertained by law, and to be informed of the nature and cause of the accusation; to be confronted with the witnesses against him; to have compulsory process for obtaining witnesses in his favor, and to have the Assistance of Counsel for his defence.

Article the ninth... In suits at common law, where the value in controversy shall exceed twenty dollars, the right of trial by jury shall be preserved, and no fact tried by a jury, shall be otherwise re-examined in any Court of the United States, than according to the rules of the common law.

Article the tenth........ Excessive bail shall not be required, nor excessive fines imposed, nor cruel and unusual punishments inflicted.

Article the eleventh. The enumeration in the Constitution, of certain rights, shall not be construed to deny or disparage others retained by the people.

Article the twelfth. The powers not delegated to the United States by the Constitution, nor prohibited by it to the States, are reserved to the States respectively, or to the people.

ATTEST

Frederick Augustus Muhlenberg, Speaker of the House of Representatives.

John Adams, Vice President of the United States, and President of the Senate.

John Beckley, Clerk of the House of Representatives.

Sam. A. Otis Secretary of the Senate.

Virginia

General Assembly begun and held at the Capitol in the City of Richmond on Monday the seventeenth of October in the Year of our Lord One thousand seven hundred and ninety one.

25th of October 1791

Resolved that the first article of the Amendment proposed by Congress to the Constitution of the United States be ratified by this Commonwealth.

November 3d 1791
Agreed to by the Senate

John Pride S.S.

Thomas Matthews Sr. H.D.

Monday the 5th of December 1791

Resolved that the second article of the Amendments proposed by Congress to the Constitution of the United States be ratified by this Commonwealth.

December 15th 1791
Agreed to by the Senate

John Pride S.S.

Thomas Matthews Sr. H.D.

Monday the 5th of December 1791

Resolved that the third article of the Amendments proposed by Congress to the Constitution of the United States be ratified by this Commonwealth.

December 15th 1791
Agreed to by the Senate

John Pride S.S.

Thomas Matthews Sr. H.D.

Monday the 5th of December 1791

Resolved that the fourth article of the Amendments proposed by Congress to the Constitution of the United States be ratified by this Commonwealth.

December 15th 1791
Agreed to by the Senate

John Pride S.S.

Thomas Matthews Sr. H.D.

Monday the 5th of December 1791

Resolved that the fifth article of the Amendments proposed by Congress to the Constitution of the United States be ratified by this Commonwealth.

December 15th 1791
Agreed to by the Senate

John Pride S.S.

Thomas Matthews Sr. H.D.

Monday the 5th of December 1791

Resolved that the sixth article of the Amendments proposed by Congress to the Constitution of the United States be ratified by this Commonwealth.

December 15th 1791
Agreed to by the Senate

John Pride S.S.

Thomas Matthews Sr. H.D.

Monday the 5th of December 1791

Resolved that the seventh article of the Amendments proposed by Congress to the Constitution of the United States be ratified by this Commonwealth.

December 15th 1791
Agreed to by the Senate

John Pride S.S.

Thomas Matthews Sr. H.D.

Monday the 5th of December 1791

Resolved that the eighth article of the Amendments proposed by Congress to the Constitution of the United States be ratified by this Commonwealth.

December 15th 1791
Agreed to by the Senate

John Pride S.S.

Thomas Matthews Sr. H.D.

Monday the 5th of December 1791

Resolved that the ninth article of the Amendments proposed by Congress to the Constitution of the United States be ratified by this Commonwealth.

December 15th 1791
Agreed to by the Senate

John Pride S.S.

Thomas Matthews Sr. H.D.

Monday the 5th of December 1791

Resolved that the tenth article of the Amendments proposed by Congress to the Constitution of the United States be ratified by this Commonwealth.

December 15th 1791
Agreed to by the Senate

John Pride S.S.

Thomas Matthews Sr. H.D.

Monday the 5th of December 1791

Resolved that the eleventh article of the Amendments proposed by Congress to the Constitution of the United States be ratified by this Commonwealth.

December 15th 1791
Agreed to by the Senate

John Pride S.S.

Thomas Matthews Sr. H.D.

Monday the 5th of December 1791

Resolved that the twelfth article of the Amendments proposed by Congress to the Constitution of the United States be ratified by this Commonwealth.

December 15th 1791
Agreed to by the Senate

John Pride S.S.

Thomas Matthews Sr. H.D.

Document 6. Virginia Ratification of the Bill of Rights, December 15, 1791. [National Archives]

Thirty-ninth Congress of the United States, at the first session, begun and held at the City of Washington, in the District of Columbia, on Monday the fourth day of December, one thousand eight hundred and sixty-five.

Joint Resolution proposing an amendment to the Constitution of the United States.

Be it resolved by the Senate and House of Representatives of the United States of America in Congress assembled, (two-thirds of both Houses concurring,) That the following article be proposed to the legislatures of the several States as an amendment to the Constitution of the United States, which, when ratified by three-fourths of said legislatures, shall be valid as part of the Constitution, namely:

Article XIV.

Section 1. All persons born or naturalized in the United States, and subject to the jurisdiction thereof, are citizens of the United States and of the State wherein they reside. No State shall make or enforce any law which shall abridge the privileges or immunities of citizens of the United States; nor shall any State deprive any person of life, liberty, or property, without due process of law; nor deny to any person within its jurisdiction the equal protection of the laws.

Section 2. Representatives shall be apportioned among the several States according to their respective numbers, counting the whole number of persons in each State, excluding Indians not taxed. But when the right to vote at any election for the choice of electors for President and Vice President of the United States, Representatives in Congress, the Executive and Judicial officers of a State, or the members of the Legislature thereof, is denied to any of the male inhabitants of such State, being twenty-one years of age, and citizens of the United States, or in any way abridged, except for participation in rebellion, or other crimes, the basis of representation therein shall be reduced in the proportion which the number of such male citizens shall bear to the whole number of male citizens twenty-one years of age in such State.

Section 3. No person shall be a Senator or Representative in Congress, or elector of President and Vice President, or hold any office, civil or military, under the United States, or under any State, who, having previously taken an oath, as a member of Congress, or as an officer of the United States, or as a member of any State legislature, or as an executive or judicial officer of any State, to support the Constitution of the United States, shall have engaged in insurrection or rebellion against the same, or given aid or comfort to the enemies thereof. But Congress may by a vote of two-thirds of each House, remove such disability.

Section 4. The validity of the public debt of the United States authorized by law, including debts incurred for payment of pensions and bounties for services in suppressing insurrection or rebellion, shall not be questioned. But neither the United States nor any State shall assume or pay any debt or obligation incurred in aid of insurrection or rebellion against the United States, or any claim for the loss or emancipation of any slave; but all such debts, obligations and claims shall be held illegal and void.

Section 5. The Congress shall have power to enforce, by appropriate legislation, the provisions of this article.

Attest.

Edw. McPherson.
Clerk of the House of Representatives.

J. W. Forney
Secretary of the Senate.

Schuyler Colfax
Speaker of the House of Representatives.

La Fayette S. Foster
President of the Senate pro tempore.

Document 7b. Fourteenth Amendment to the Constitution, June 16, 1866. [National Archives]

103

W. G. Wyly   Associate Justice

His Honor the Chief Justice pronounced the judg"
"ment and decree of the court in the following
case:

Butchers Benevolent Association
    of New Orleans
       vs
The Crescent City Live Stock Landing
and Slaughter House Co

           No 2505

It is ordered that the Re-hearing applied for in
this case be Refused.

Petition for Writ of Error

The United States of America

State of Louisiana   Parish of Orleans

To the Honorable Joseph P. Bradley Associate Justice of the
Supreme Court of the United States:

The petition of the Benevolent Butchers Association of New Orleans
an incorporation under the Special Corporation Law of Louisiana,
through its President Paul Esteben Plaintiff in a cause wherein
the Crescent City Live Stock Landing & Slaughter House Co. is defendant:
plaintiff Respectfully represents That he is aggrieved by a
final judgment in the Supreme Court of the State of Louisiana in above named suit bearing date, the 9th. day of
May instant and that petitioner exhibits to your Honor
a Copy of the Record of the said cause with the opinions
& decree of the said Supreme Court therein annexed to this

Document 8a. Petition for a writ of error in the Slaughterhouse cases, May 13, 1870. [National Archives]

petition as exhibit A.

That it appears on the face of the said Record that your petitioner claimed a right, privilege & title under the Constitution of the United States, & especially under the Fourteenth Amendment thereof, for itself as a Corporation & for all the members thereof individually and collectively to labor in their vocation of Butchers, and in the business of dealing in & landing of Live Stock & Slaughter House business on equal terms & conditions with other Citizens of the United States, wherever & wheresoever said business was allowed under the laws of the State or the United States:

But that against common right & the right of Plaintiffs, these petitioners, the Legislature of Louisiana did grant to seventeen persons incorporated as the said Crescent City Live Stock Landing & Slaughter House Company, the sole & exclusive privileges of conducting the Live Stock Landing & Slaughter House business within the limits & privileges of the said Act & did make it unlawful for any person or persons to land, keep or Slaughter, Cattle, horses, sheep, swine or other animals, or to have any Stock Landing, yards, pens, Slaughter house or abattoirs at any point or place within the Parishes of Orleans, Jefferson or St. Bernard or within the Corporate limits of the City of New Orleans, other than those of the said Corporation, & made it unlawful for any person or persons to conduct or to carry on said business, and did require that all places for carrying on said business should be no other than those of said Company, & did require that all animals designed for sale & Slaughter in said Parishes should be landed at the wharves & sheltered & kept, at the houses & yards of said Corporation, & fixed a tariff of burdensome charges therefor

Document 8b. Petition for a writ of error in the Slaughterhouse cases, May 13, 1870. [National Archives]

105 contrary to common right and the Constitution of the United States as aforesaid:

And your petitioners aver that in the said cause was set up, the said constitutional right, title & privilege, but that said Court overruled & determined adversely to the same, thereby establishing and maintaining an odious, oppressive & mischievous monopoly against Common right & the law of the Constitution.

Wherefore they pray respectfully of your Honor to allow a writ of Error to the Supreme Court of the United States; to sign a citation to the defendant in said cause and to approve the bond here with submitted; and for such order as may further to justice & right in the premises appertain.

(Signed)   Fellows & Mills
(Signed)   Cotton & Levy

Writ of Error allowed
May 13th. 1870
(Signed) Josep. Bradley
Apo: Justice Sup. Ct. U.S.

Filed May 16th. 1870
(Signed) M.P. Julian Dy Clerk
Sup. Court State of La

~~~~~~~

Bond for Writ of Error
                Supreme Court of Louisiana
The Butchers Benevolent Association
of New Orleans
                vs   } No. 2505
The Crescent City Live Stock Landing
& Slaughter House Co
                Know all men by these Presents,

Document 8c. Petition for a writ of error in the Slaughterhouse cases, May 13, 1870. [National Archives]

Hon A. T. Akerman,
Attorney- General of the United States
Washington D. C.

Sir:

I have the honor to submit the following preliminary report of operations, conducted pursuant to a letter of instructions and authority addressed to me from your office under date of June 28th 1871, desiring my assistance in effecting the ends of an appropriation made by Congress for the detection and prosecution of crimes against the United States, having particularly in view certain sorts of crimes, committed in violation of the Acts of Congress approved May 31st 1870 and April 20th 1871, and which are reported to be more frequent in the South than elsewhere.

At an early stage of my investigations it became apparent that the service was one of the most arduous and hazardous nature.

In communities where the voice of the people is almost universal for the maintenance of law and order, the detection and suppression of crime is a comparatively easy task, but in localities where the masses are defective where the local police are governed by the popular prejudice, and where every stranger is looked upon with suspicion, all routine methods of detection become useless, and must be superseded by entirely new and original modes of procedure.

In accordance with the instructions contained in your letter of the 28th of June, I have selected for this service men of known capability and trust, and detailed them to such districts in the South as were said to be the field of alleged outrages. They found however that unless they went there with the apparent intention of becoming permanent residents, they could not gain the confidence of those from whom information leading to satisfactory results might be obtained, and through whose instrumentality,

Document 9b. H.C. Whitley's report to Attorney General George Williams about the Ku Klux Klan, September 29, 1871. [National Archives]

access might be had to the bands of armed men who were reported as daily committing outrages upon such citizens as chose to exercise the right of suffrage unbiased by the popular clamor. The Congressional Committee of Investigation had just been through the infected districts, and it was rumored in all directions that the country was full of government spies, and hence all strangers must be especially watched and in no case trusted.

The men were accordingly compelled to assume characters as trades people, casting about for a good business location; liquor and wine merchants traveling from place to place as agents for houses in large southern centres; pedlers, and in some instances farm-hands and laborers in search of employment, modes of procedure necessitating the consumption of much time and the expenditure of considerable sums of money. The greatest obstacle of all however was the reticence of the citizens both white and colored who had been the unfortunate victims of these outrages.

Document 9c. H.C. Whitley's report to Attorney General George Williams about the Ku Klux Klan, September 29, 1871. [National Archives]

Those who have escaped with life have had a seal put upon their lips which they dare not break upon pain of death and the dead leave nothing but their mangled corpses to tell the story of their wrongs. — I have been thus explicit in order to give you some idea of the state of the country at the time the officers first located there, and the difficulties under which they labor, and are still laboring in obtaining information. The results thus far have been fully commensurate with the time and money expended. The investigation has established the fact,— and made it susceptible of proof,— that there are in a portion of the Southern States organized bands of armed men who go in disguise upon the public highways and upon the premises of certain citizens of the United States, with intent to injure, oppress and intimidate them, and hinder the free exercise of the rights and privileges granted all citizens without distinction of race and color under the Constitution and Laws of the United States; that these bands of armed men under

the names, formerly of the "Constitutional
Union Guards" and "White Brotherhood",
but now known as the "Order of Invisible
Empire", or "Ku Klux Klan", have signs,
grips, pass words and other modes of
recognition, and a code of "signals
by sound", which are produced by
whistles, and which suffice to guide
and direct the movements of the members
without the aid of the human voice;
and that meetings of the order are
held in open fields or sequestered
woods where the approach of spies
or unfriendly parties can the more
easily be detected.

M. G. Brauer, an officer detailed
by me for the service reports, that on
the night of the 19th of July 1871 a
meeting of the "Klan" was held near
a place called Dobson's store, located
on the highway between Yorkville and
Kings Mountain, York Co. S. C.
Brauer, by supplying certain suspected
parties copiously with intoxicating
liquors the day previous, had learned
of the meeting, and as the night
in question proved favorable to his

designs, he was enabled to approach near enough to overhear a large portion of the proceedings. Among other matters he learned that all meetings of the Klan had for the present been suspended, and it was ordered that any member of the Klan who should divulge any of their operations to the Congressional Committee of Investigation then in the vicinity, should suffer death. At this same meeting the project of waylaying the Committee on its return to Washington and robbing that body of such evidence as it had accumulated, was fully discussed but not decided upon.

At a subsequent visit to Dobsons store, Mr. Brawer learned that a colored man named Roundtree, formerly residing in the vicinity had been murdered for exercising the right of suffrage independently of threats that had been made him by the Ku Klux. The affair was talked over in the store among some parties and the names of John Hicks, Thomas Deprise, one McByas and Samuel Randall given as the parties who committed the murder. The first three reside in York district, about 22 miles from Yorkville, Randall lives in North Carolina

Document 9f. H.C. Whitley's report to Attorney General George Williams about the Ku Klux Klan, September 29, 1871. [National Archives]

Mr. Bauer was unable to find any witnesses to the affair, who would testify to the occurrence.

At Spartansburgh, S.C. Mr. Bauer obtained the confidence of a member of the "Invisible Empire", and learned from him that Hugh Fowler of Laurensville S.C. was Chief of the Order in that section of the country, and that Green Brown, Elisha Shippy, Earl Smith and one Mitchel are prominent members. Working upon the information thus obtained, Mr. Bauer arrived at the organization as follows:

Hugh Fowler of Laurensville, Commander
Capt. Lials of Limestone, Captain
Frank Maple and Wm. Webster, asst. Captains.
Henry Gready, Lamp Haines, Barney Cook, Bazan Bullock James Jones, Thomas Scott, Balias Mathews, Felia Spencer, John Shippy, Dick Shippy, Green Brown, Alfred Cook, John Woods Thos Woods, May. J. V. Fauch, Randolph Brown and one McThompson, members.

He further learned that David G. Guest, son of Ex-Governor Guest was in command of the Ku Klux Klan when five men were taken from the Union Co. jail and hung by them, and

To the Senate and House of Representatives of the United States in Congress assembled—

Your Petitioners

Colored Citizens of Cleveland & vicinity, Tenn. humbly pray that the Fourteenth Amendment to the Constitution of the United States, be so enforced by "appropriate legislation that no State be, hereafter, permitted to make or enforce any law abridging our privileges or immunities as citizens of the United States.

As reasons for presenting this Petition we urge the following,—

1 Without such enforcement the first section of said Amendment is for the Colored People, virtually, a dead letter. In our own State a colored man though eligible to the office of Governor or President; is not allowed to travel in a first class R. Road car or send his children to the same school with his white neighbors'. Tennessee has never had a Common School nor can she have one till the evil of which we complain be abated.

2. The deprivation of these, and others of our rights as Citizens is a contempt to our race, a great injury to us individually, and at the same time a damage to the white race, as well. To instance only one item— not a few of the public white Schools about us have been continued this year only two and one-half months.— If the Public School Fund in these sparsely populated States, must; to gratify a slavery-engendered prejudice, be divided, it will follow with unfailing certainty, that the illiteracy of whites as well as blacks will increase continually.

3. We petition not for any favor but for the undisturbed enjoyment of our chartered rights. The organic law of our whole land knows nothing of white citizens or black citizens, as such

Document 10a. Petition for the enforcement of the Fourteenth Amendment, January 19, 1874. [National Archives]

but decrees that all born or naturalized in the land are equal before the law. If a State be tolerated in shutting the colored man out of the public schools it might with equal reason be allowed to deny to him the right to testify or vote.

4.   We would remind our Rulers that in those dark days when a gigantic Rebellion threatened the national life, the colored men of Tennessee, so loved liberty, that while yet slaves and with no promise even of personal freedom for their race, they rushed by thousands into the Federal armies. We do not complain that the disabilities of the men we then fought, are removed, but we confess ourselves unable to understand on what principle of equity or expediency it is that our own disabilities are allowed to remain. We do not question the policy of the General Government being magnanimous to its enemies, but we must doubt the wisdom of its tolerating States in visiting insult and injury upon its friends.

5   We urge our Petition with the more of assurance since all we claim was pledged us in both of the Party Platforms of 1872 - platforms voted upon by more than six millions of American freemen. We ask respectfully but with earnestness, and persistently, that the pledge thus solemnly given by the nation be redeemed.

Names   Names

Anthony Coxtis.
Geo. T. Warrom.
Mofos Brown
Cyze Parks
Gig Calomay.
Scott Peyton.
Geo Christmas.

Document 10b. Petition for the enforcement of the Fourteenth
Amendment, January 19, 1874. [National Archives]

IN THE

Supreme Court of the United States

OCTOBER TERM, 1946

ARCH R. EVERSON,
Appellant,

against

BOARD OF EDUCATION OF THE TOWNSHIP OF
EWING, IN THE COUNTY OF MERCER, *et al.,*
Appellees.

No. 52.

ON APPEAL FROM THE COURT OF ERRORS AND APPEALS OF THE
STATE OF NEW JERSEY

BRIEF OF AMERICAN CIVIL LIBERTIES UNION
AS *AMICUS CURIAE*

Interest of American Civil Liberties Union

This brief is filed with consent of the parties. The American Civil Liberties Union is a nonprofit, nonpartisan organization having a nationwide membership of persons of all religious views and sects including citizens of New Jersey. It is devoted to the preservation and protection of the fundamental liberties guaranteed citizens of this country by Federal and State constitutions. It believes in the historic, basic American doctrine of separation of church and state and that only by its steadfast and

Document 11a. Amicus curiae brief of the American Civil Liberties Union in *Everson v. Board of Education of Ewing Township, New Jersey*, November 14, 1946. [National Archives]

strict observance can the religious freedom of all the people be assured.

We wish it clearly understood that in filing this brief we do not, expressly or by implication, attack or criticize the principles or practices of any religious organization or disparage parochial or private schools for those whose consciences or preferences prompt them to use such means for the education of their children. We respect the convictions of those who believe it desirable that a school which combines secular and religious instruction is best adapted to the proper development of their children.

What we say here we would repeat with equal emphasis in respect of schools or institutions of any religious denomination or sect.

Our sole concern is with the constitutionality of the appropriation of public moneys for transportation of children to private, sectarian schools.

Statement of the Case

The facts are simple, undisputed. Appellee Board of Education of Ewing Township, New Jersey, in September, 1942, adopted a resolution providing for "transportation of pupils of Ewing to the Trenton and Pennington High and Trenton Catholic Schools by way of public carriers as in recent years". It agreed to pay, for that current school year, the cost of transportation to such Catholic parochial schools. Part of the agreed sum was paid, the balance remaining unpaid because of this suit. Transportation was by public carrier buses. The Board reimbursed Township parents for bus fares, between that township and Trenton, paid by their children attending the four Trenton Catholic parochial schools. These schools, located outside of the Ewing school district, were maintained by

Document 11b. Amicus curiae brief of the American Civil Liberties Union in *Everson v. Board of Education of Ewing Township, New Jersey*, November 14, 1946. [National Archives]

the parish and parents, religion was taught there, and a Catholic priest was school superintendent.

The Board's resolution was based on a New Jersey statute (Rev. Stat. 18:14-8, as amended by Chap. 191, N. J. Laws of 1941) which provides:

> "18:14-8. Whenever in any district there are children living remote from *any* schoolhouse, the board of education of the district may make rules and contracts for the transportation of such children to and from school, *including the transportation of children to and from school other than a public school, except such school as is operated for profit in whole or in part.*
>
> *When any school district provides any transportation for public school children to and from school, transportation from any point in such established school route to any other point in such established school route shall be supplied to school children residing in such school district in going to and from school other than a public school, except such school as is operated for profit in whole or in part.*"
> (Italics ours.)

The amendments of 1941 changed "the schoolhouse" to "any schoolhouse", and added the italicized matter.

On application of appellant, resident and taxpayer of Ewing Township, a writ of certiorari was issued by the New Jersey Supreme Court to review the legality of the resolution. Appellant urged the resolution and statute were illegal as violating various provisions of the New Jersey Constitution (Art. I, Pars. 3, 4, 19, 20, and Art. IV, Sec. 7, Par. 6), and the Fourteenth Amendment of the Federal Constitution.

The New Jersey Supreme Court (one Justice dissenting) set aside the resolution, holding it violated Art. IV,

Document 11c. Amicus curiae brief of the American Civil Liberties Union in *Everson v. Board of Education of Ewing Township, New Jersey*, November 14, 1946. [National Archives]

Sec. 7, Par. 6 of the State Constitution providing that the fund for the support of free schools may be appropriated only to the support of public free schools and not for any other purpose under any pretense (132 N. J. L. 98; R. pp. 34-41).

On appeal, the New Jersey Court of Errors and Appeals reversed and dismissed the writ on the ground the resolution and statute did not contravene the State or Federal Constitutions. Three judges dissented (133 N. J. L. 350; R. pp. 45-62). That Court denied reargument, but allowed this appeal (R. pp. 63, 65).

Appellant assigns as error that the resolution and statute contravene the Fourteenth Amendment in authorizing the gift and use of public funds in aid of private and sectarian schools and the taking of private property for a private purpose or private persons and constitute legislation respecting the establishment of religion and authorizing support of religious tenets by taxation (R. pp. 64-65).

POINT I

The statute and resolution are violative of the Federal constitutional guarantees respecting religious freedom and the fundamental doctrine of separation of church and state inherent therein.

We respectfully submit that the use of public moneys to transport children attending parochial schools is in aid and support of such schools and of religious institutions and tenets, and that the statute and resolution authorizing such expenditures violate the fundamental American principle of separation of church and state and the constitutional prohibition respecting the establishment of religion.

Document 11d. Amicus curiae brief of the American Civil Liberties Union in *Everson v. Board of Education of Ewing Township, New Jersey*, November 14, 1946. [National Archives]

Whereas Maj. Gen. U.S. Grant of the Army of the United States on the 17th day of December 1862 issued the following general order

HEADQUARTERS 13TH ARMY CORPS,
Department of the Tennessee,
Oxford Missippi, December 17, 1862.
GENERAL ORDER NO. 11.

The Jews, as a class, violating every regulation of trade established by the Treasury Department, also department orders, are hereby expelled from the department within twenty-four (24) hours from the receipt of this order by Post Commanders.

They will see that all this class of people are furnished with passes and required to leave, and any one returning after such notification will be arrested and held in confinement until an opportunity occurs of sending them out as prisoners, unless furnished with permits from these headquarters.

No passes will be given these people to visit headquarters for the purpose of making personal application for trade permits.

By order of   Major General GRANT.
JOHN A. RAWLINS, A. A. G.
Official—J. LOVELL, Captain and A. A. G.

and whereas by virtue of said order the Jews as a class — who claim to be loyal citizens of the United States, have been expelled from the city of Paducah Kentucky — and have been driven from their business and homes by the military authority, without any specific charges having been made against them, or any opportunity se given them to meet the vague and general charges set forth in said order; therefore

Resolved. By the senate of the United States that the said order of Maj. Gen. Grant, expelling the jews as a class from the department, of which he is in command is condemned, as illegal, tyrannis Tyranical, cruel and unjust; [And the President is requested to countermand the same]

Powell to strike out last clause

37 Cong. }
3 Sess. }

Resolution
by Mr Powell in
relation to an order
issued by Major Genl.
U. S. Grant, expelling
Jews from the depart-
ment of which he
is in Command &c.

1863 Jany. 5. Submitted.
" Jany. 9th Resumed — Clark
to be indefinitely
Powell ~~fly J & N~~ Hale to
lie on table — Powell fa Y & N
yeas — 30 Nays 7 —

United States of America, ss:

The President of the United States of America,

(SEAL)

To the Honorable the Judges of the ___District___ ——————
Court of the United States for the ___Southern___ ——————
District of ___West Virginia,___ ——————————

GREETING:

Whereas, lately in the ___District___ ——————— Court of the United States for the ___Southern___ — District of ___West Virginia,___ ——————— before you, or some of you, in a cause between Walter Barnette, Paul Stull and Lucy McClure, Plaintiffs, and The West Virginia State Board of Education, Composed of Hon. W. W. Trent, President, et al., Defendants, No. 242, wherein the decree of the said District Court, entered in said cause on the 6th day of October, A. D. 1942, is in the following words, vis:

"This cause coming on to be heard on motion for interlocutory injunction before the undersigned constituting a District Court of three judges convened according to statute; and being heard upon the bill of complaint, as amended, the motion to dismiss and the arguments of counsel; and being submitted for final decree; and the Court having made findings of fact and conclusions of law, which are filed herewith:

Now, therefore, for reasons set forth in the written opinion herewith filed, it is ordered, adjudged and decreed that the defendants, the West Virginia State Board of Education and the individual members thereof, and all boards, officials, teachers and other persons in any way subject to the jurisdiction of said West Virginia State Board of Education, be, and they are hereby, restrained and enjoined from requiring the children of the plaintiffs, or any other children having religious scruples against such action, to salute the flag of the United States, or any other flag, or from expelling such children from school for failure to salute it; and that plaintiffs recover of defendants the costs of suit to be taxed by the clerk of the court."

as by the inspection of the transcript of the record, ————————————————— ———————————————————————————————— *of the said* **District** ———— *Court, which was brought into the SUPREME COURT OF THE UNITED STATES by virtue of* **an appeal,** ————————————————————————

agreeably to the act of Congress, ———————————————————— ———————————————— *in such case made and provided, fully and at large appears.*

And whereas, *in the present term of October, in the year of our Lord one thousand nine hundred and* **forty-two** ———— *, the said cause came on to be heard before the said SUPREME COURT, on the said transcript of record, and was argued by counsel:*

On consideration whereof, *It is now here ordered,* ———— *adjudged,* **and decreed** ———————— *by this Court that the* **decree** —— *of the said* **District** ———— *Court, in this cause be, and the same is hereby,* **affirmed with costs.**

June 14, 1943.

Document 13c. Mandate in *West Virginia v. Barnette*, June 14, 1943. [National Archives].

You, therefore, are hereby commanded that such ~~execution and~~ ═══════════

proceedings be had in said cause, ═══════════════════════════════

═══════════════════════════ as according to right and justice, and the laws

of the United States, ought to be had, the said **appeal** ═══════════════

notwithstanding.

HARLAN F. STONE,

~~Witness~~, the Honorable ~~CHARLES E. HUGHES~~, Chief Justice of the United

States, the **twenty-first** ── day of **July** ─────── , in the year of our

Lord one thousand nine hundred and forty-**three.**

Costs of **plaintiffs**

Clerk_____ $) Paid by
)
~~Printing record~~──── $)
)
Attorney_____ $) **defendants**
)
$)

Charles Elmore Cropley
Clerk of the Supreme Court of the United States.

Supreme Court of the United States

File No. _____

No. **591** ──, *October Term,* 194**2**

The West Virginia State Board

of Education, etc., et al.,

vs.

Walter Barnette, Paul Stull and

Lucy McClure.

MANDATE

U. S. GOVERNMENT PRINTING OFFICE   2540055

Document 13d. Mandate in *West Virginia v. Barnette*, June 14, 1943. [National Archives].

IN SENATE OF THE UNITED STATES.

FEBRUARY 24, 1825.

Mr. DICKERSON, from the Select Committee to whom was referred the petition of Thomas Cooper, President of the South Carolina College,

REPORTED:

That the petitioner states, that, in the month of April, 1800, at the city of Philadelphia, he was indicted and found guilty of having printed and published what was alleged to be a libel against Mr. John Adams, the then President of the United States, under the act commonly called the sedition law, passed the 14th of July, 1798; the second section whereof runs as follows, viz:—" *And be it further enacted,* That if any person shall write, print, utter, or publish, or shall cause or procure to be written, printed, uttered, or published, or shall, knowingly or willingly, assist or aid in writing, printing, uttering, or publishing, any false, scandalous, and malicious writing or writings, against the Government of the United States, or either House of Congress of the United States, or the President of the United States, with an intent to defame the Government of the United States, or either House of the said Congress, or the President, or to bring them, or either of them, into contempt or disrepute, or to excite against them, or either, or any, of them, the hatred of the good people of the United States, &c. then such person being thereof convicted, before any court of the United States having jurisdiction thereof, shall be punished by fine, not exceeding two thousand dollars, and by imprisonment not exceeding two years." He further states, that, under this section, he was sentenced, upon a conviction of having printed and published the above alleged libel, to pay a fine of four hundred dollars, and to be imprisoned during six months. He further states, that, on the day when his imprisonment expired, he paid into the hands of John Hall, Esq. Marshal for the District of Pennsylvania, the aforesaid fine of four hundred dollars, for the use of the Treasury of the United States. He further states, that the law under which he was convicted, called the sedition law, was an unconstitutional law, such as the legislature that passed it had no right to enact; and that the fine so exacted from and paid by him, was illegally exacted and ought not to be retained. He therefore prays, that the fine so paid by him may be restored, with interest.

Document 14a. Petition for restoration of Thomas Cooper's fine, February 24, 1825. [National Archives]

The Committee are of opinion, that the prayer of the petitioner is reasonable, and ought to be granted; and submit the following resolution:

Resolved, That the prayer of the petition ought to be granted.

Heremiert Cockers Petition
S. Orl. 249 n° 30

Circuit Court of the United States for the Pennsylvania District: *April Term*, 1800.

The UNITED STATES
vs.
THOMAS COOPER.   } Indictment for a seditious libel.

The Grand Inquest of the United States of America, in and for the Pennsylvania District, upon their respective oaths and affirmations, do present, that Thomas Cooper, late of the District of Pennsylvania, attorney at law, being a person of wicked and turbulent disposition, designing and intending to defame the President of the United States, and to bring him into contempt and disrepute, and to excite against him the hatred of the good people of the United States; on the second day of November, in the year one thousand seven hundred and ninety-nine, in the district aforesaid, and within the jurisdiction of this Court, wickedly and maliciously did write, print, and publish, a false, scandalous, and malicious writing, against the said President of the United States, of the tenor and effect following; that is to say: "Nor do I, [himself the said Thomas Cooper meaning,] see any impropriety in making this request of Mr. Adams; [meaning John Adams, Esquire, President of the United States;] at that time he had just entered into office: He [meaning the said President of the United States,] was hardly in the infancy of political mistake; even those who doubted his capacity, [meaning the capacity of the said President of the United States,] thought well of his [meaning the said President of the United States] intentions." And also the false, scandalous, and malicious words, of the tenor and effect following; that is to say: "Nor were we, [meaning the People of the United States,] yet saddled with the expense of a permanent navy, or threatened under his [meaning the said President's] auspices with the existence of a standing army. Our credit, [meaning the credit of the United States,] was not yet reduced so low, as to borrow money at eight per cent. in time of peace, while the unnecessary violence of official expressions might justly have provoked a war." And also the false, scandalous, and malicious words, of the tenor and effect following; that is to say: "Mr. Adams, [meaning the said President of the United States,] had not yet projected his [the said President of the United States meaning] embassies to Prussia, Russia, and the Sublime Porte; nor had he, [the said President of the United States meaning,] yet interfered as President of the United States, to influence the decisions of a court of justice—

a stretch of authority which the monarch of Great Britain would have shrunk from; an interference without precedent against law, and against mercy. This melancholy case of Jonathan Robins, a native citizen of America, forcibly impressed by the British, and delivered up with the advice of **Mr. Adams**, [meaning the said President of the United States,] to the mock trial of a British Court Martial, had not yet astonished the republican citizens of this free country, [meaning the United States of America;] a case too little known, but of which the people, [meaning the people of the United States of America,] ought to be fully apprized before the election, and they shall be"—to the great scandal of the President of the United States; to the evil example of others, in like case, offending against the form of the act of Congress of the United States, in such case made and provided, and against the peace and dignity of the said United States.

W. RAWLE, *Attorney General.*

To this indictment, Thomas Cooper put in the plea of not guilty, and also pleaded the truth of the facts in justification.

Upon this indictment and plea, Thomas Cooper was found guilty; and the court sentenced him to pay a fine of four hundred dollars; to be imprisoned for six months; and, at the end of that period, to find surety for his good behaviour, himself in a thousand, and two sureties, in five hundred dollars each.

Sixty-fifth Congress of the United States of America;

At the First Session,

Begun and held at the City of Washington on Monday, the second day of April, one thousand nine hundred and seventeen.

AN ACT

To punish acts of interference with the foreign relations, the neutrality, and the foreign commerce of the United States, to punish espionage, and better to enforce the criminal laws of the United States, and for other purposes.

Be it enacted by the Senate and House of Representatives of the United States of America in Congress assembled:

TITLE I.

ESPIONAGE.

SECTION 1. That (a) whoever, for the purpose of obtaining information respecting the national defense with intent or reason to believe that the information to be obtained is to be used to the injury of the United States, or to the advantage of any foreign nation, goes upon, enters, flies over, or otherwise obtains information concerning any vessel, aircraft, work of defense, navy yard, naval station, submarine base, coaling station, fort, battery, torpedo station, dockyard, canal, railroad, arsenal, camp, factory, mine, telegraph, telephone, wireless, or signal station, building, office, or other place connected with the national defense, owned or constructed, or in progress of construction by the United States or under the control of the United States, or of any of its officers or agents, or within the exclusive jurisdiction of the United States, or any place in which any vessel, aircraft, arms, munitions, or other materials or instruments for use in time of war are being made, prepared, repaired, or stored, under any contract or agreement with the United States, or with any person on behalf of the United States, or otherwise on behalf of the United States, or or any of the rights or obligations of the United States under any treaty or the law of nations, shall be fined not more than $1,000 or imprisoned not more than two years, or both.

Sec. 23. Nothing contained in this title shall be held to repeal or impair any existing provisions of law regulating search and the issue of search warrants.

TITLE XII.

USE OF MAILS.

Section 1. Every letter, writing, circular, postal card, picture, print, engraving, photograph, newspaper, pamphlet, book, or other publication, matter, or thing, of any kind, in violation of any of the provisions of this Act is hereby declared to be nonmailable matter and shall not be conveyed in the mails or delivered from any post office or by any letter carrier: *Provided*, That nothing in this Act shall be so construed as to authorize any person other than an employee of the Dead Letter Office, duly authorized thereto, or other person upon a search warrant authorized by law, to open any letter not addressed to himself.

Sec. 2. Every letter, writing, circular, postal card, picture, print, engraving, photograph, newspaper, pamphlet, book, or other publication, matter or thing, of any kind, containing any matter advocating or urging treason, insurrection, or forcible resistance to any law of the United States, is hereby declared to be nonmailable.

Sec. 3. Whoever shall use or attempt to use the mails or Postal Service of the United States for the transmission of any matter declared by this title to be nonmailable, shall be fined not more than $5,000 or imprisoned not more than five years, or both. Any person violating any provision of this title may be tried and punished either in the district in which the unlawful matter or publication was mailed, or to which it was carried by mail for delivery according to the direction thereon, or in which it was caused to be delivered by mail to the person to whom it was addressed.

TITLE XIII.

GENERAL PROVISIONS.

Section 1. The term "United States" as used in this Act includes the Canal Zone and all territory and waters, continental or insular, subject to the jurisdiction of the United States.

Sec. 2. The several courts of first instance in the Philippine Islands and the district court of the Canal Zone shall have jurisdiction of offenses under this Act committed within their respective districts, and concurrent jurisdiction with the district courts of the United States of offenses under this Act committed upon the high seas, and of conspiracies to commit such offenses, as defined by section thirty-seven of the Act entitled "An Act to codify, revise, and amend

American Secret Service Men Fathom Inner most Secrets of the Sinn Fein Revolutionists.

PLANS FOR A REVOLT FOUND ON MELLOWES.

Operative Flynn Gives Out Text of an Artfully Worded Letter Welsh Tried to Destroy.

[BY A. P. NIGHT WIRE.]

NEW YORK, Nov. 11.—Details of the plans of Sinn Fein leaders for the insurrection in Ireland which administered in the Easter Monday rain of last year, together with information relative to the landing on the Irish coast of Sir Roger Casement, were recounted in a communication found in the possession of "Liam" Mellowes, Irish revolutionist arrested here several weeks ago and made public today by William J. Flynn, chief of the United States secret service.

SUGAR AVAILABLE FOR EASTERN NEEDS.

[BY A. P. NIGHT WIRE.]

WASHINGTON, Nov. 11.—More than 2,310,000 pounds of beet sugar, held for foreign relief before the food administration was informed yesterday, will be available for shipment this week to the consumption East.

ANTHRAX AGAIN.

Three Infected Steers are Slaughtered; Because They were Afflicted.

[BY A. P. NIGHT WIRE.]

OVER FORTY MILLIONS FOR RED CROSS WORK.

[BY A. P. NIGHT WIRE.]

WASHINGTON, Nov. 11.—

GARFIELD WASTES COAL AND ELECTRIC LIGHTS.

Conservation of Fuel is Apparently Forgotten at Washington Office.

[BY DIRECT WIRE—EXCLUSIVE DISPATCH.]

WASHINGTON BUREAU OF THE TIMES, Nov. 11.—

PROPOSED GAS PRICE RAISE IS PROTESTED.

[BY A. P. NIGHT WIRE.]

SAN FRANCISCO, Nov. 11.—

Weds an Albanian Prince.

Ex-wife of Frank Gould.

Mrs Helen Kelly Thomas, widow of Ralph H. Thomas and once the wife of Frank Gould, was married to Prince Nourreddin Z. Vlora of Albania by a clerk in the marriage license bureau in New York City. The bride is the grand-daughter of the late Eugene Kelly a great financier of his day.

OUR MILITARY EXPERTS ANALYZE WAR MOVES.

Kerensky's Return to Power Expected. Italian Troops are Retiring to Shorter Battle Line.

[BY DIRECT WIRE—EXCLUSIVE DISPATCH.]

WASHINGTON BUREAU OF THE TIMES, Nov. 11.—

SHORTER BATTLE LINE.

HUGE FOODSTUFF CACHE IS FOUND IN NEW YORK.

Part of the Goods, Valued at $73,000,000, Belongs to Germans.

[BY A. P. NIGHT WIRE.]

NEW YORK, Nov. 11.—

FINLAND IS AT WAR; SAILOR IS THE RULER.

[BY ATLANTIC CABLE AND A. P.]

HELSINGFORS, Nov. 11.—

GERMAN REVOLUTIONARY MOVE STIRS BRAZILIANS.

[BY ATLANTIC CABLE AND A. P.]

RIO (Brazil), Nov. 8.—

SPEED UP INQUIRY INTO PHONE STRIKE.

MEDIATION BOARD HELD SUNDAY SESSION.

Offensive by Diaz.

(Continued from First Page)

SHIPWRIGHTS ARE EXEMPT.

But Only When Engaged on Government Work.

Gen. Crowder Explains New Draft Rules.

Provision Intended to Speed up Shipbuilding.

[BY A. P. NIGHT WIRE.]

WASHINGTON, Nov. 11.—Gen. Crowder has issued the following statement.

FOR THE Y.M.C.A.

VON DANDL IS NEW BAVARIAN PREMIER.

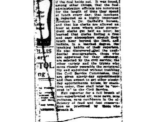

Wastes Coal.

(Continued from Second Page)

(Continued on Fourth Page.)

Document 16. "Garfield Wastes Coal and Electric Lights," *Los Angeles Daily Times*, November 12, 1917. [National Archives]

190317-227

May 15, 1918.

Hon. Hooper Alexander,
    U. S. Attorney,
        Atlanta, Ga.

S i r :

        In response to your communication of May 11th,
1918, regarding the Kingdom News, the instructions of the
Chief of the Bureau of Investigation to which you refer
are concerned with No. 2 of Volume 1 of the Kingdom News
of the International Bible Students Association, dated
New York City April 15, 1918, headed "The Finished Mystery
and Why Suppressed".

        It is the opinion of the Department that in so
far as this is distributed to the regular, recognized
members of the International Bible Students Association,
it may be treated as a bulletin of information from the
association to its members. Its distribution outside
of this membership, however, is plainly for propaganda
purposes and, taken in connection with The Finished Mystery,
may be considered as anti-war propaganda.

        The anti-war features of The Finished Mystery are
no doubt familiar to you, and can be easily obtained from
an examination of that book. That book plainly treated
participation in war as irreligious, un-Christian, a violation
of the word of God and an adherence to the purposes and designs
of Satan. This number of the Kingdom News practically does
the same thing, and the two publications are to be treated
as a part of the same propaganda, violating Section 3, Title
I of the Espionage Act.

        This number of the Kingdom News contains some
mis-statements of fact. The intimation that the suppression
of The Finished Mystery is due to religious persecution
instituted by the regular clergy to the Russellites is,
of course, entirely false. The statement that the censor
committee of the Intelligence Section of the War Department
suggested the removal of pages 247 to 253 is not correct.

                            Respectfully,
                            For The Attorney General,
                            (Signed) JOHN LORD O'BRIAN

                            Special Assistant to
                            The Attorney General.

Document 18. Poster, "True Blue," 1919. [National Archives]

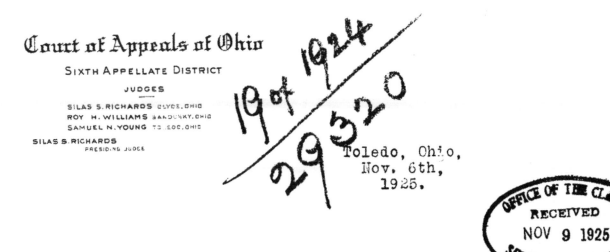

Court of Appeals of Ohio

SIXTH APPELLATE DISTRICT

JUDGES

SILAS S. RICHARDS CLYDE, OHIO
ROY H. WILLIAMS SANDUSKY, OHIO
SAMUEL N. YOUNG TOLEDO, OHIO

SILAS S. RICHARDS
PRESIDING JUDGE

19 of 1924
29320

Toledo, Ohio,
Nov. 6th,
1925.

Clerk, Supreme Court of
the United States,
Washington, D. C.

My dear Clerk:

I am informed that the United States Supreme
Court has rendered a decision in a case defining free
speech. The case was that of a conspicuous, radical
Socialist prosecuted under the New York criminal
anarchy law and the plea of defense was the constitutional guaranty of free speech.

The excerpt of the decision which is before
me is so brief, only two or three lines, that it conveys very little information and I should appreciate
very much a citation as to where this decision may be
found.

Thanking you in advance, I am

Very truly yours,

S. N. Young

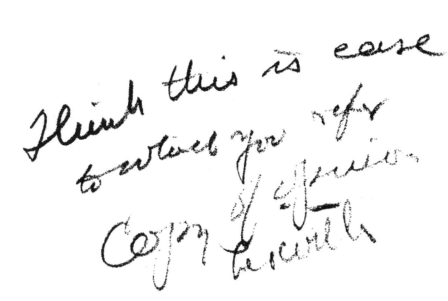

Document 19. Samuel Young's letter to the Clerk of the Supreme Court
about *Gitlow v. New York*, November 6, 1925. [National Archives]

tiffs, and Herrick, Langdon, Sandblom, and Belin for defendants, make the following Pre-Trial Stipulation pursuant to the order of the Court entered May 24, 1966.

I

This action was commenced alleging jurisdiction conferred by 42 USCA 1983, plaintiffs contending they were suspended from defendant school district for participating in conduct privileged by Amendment Fourteen on the U. S. Constitution, to wit: wearing black cloth arm bands to express a political idea. Plaintiffs seek an order restraining defendants from disciplining them so as to deprive them of their rights to free speech; and seeking nominal damages.

II

The following facts are hereby stipulated as true and undisputed in this action.

a. Prior to December 16, 1965, defendant Peterson and defendants Rowley, Betz, Jackson, Bowen, and Wetter met in their capacities as officials of defendant district and decided that students of defendant district would be prohibited from wearing black arm bands while in school.

b. Prior to December 16, 1965, the aforestated prohibition was announced to students and employees of defendant district.

c. On December 16, 1965, plaintiffs Christopher Eckhardt and Mary Beth Tinker wore black arm bands while attending schools in defendant district and were told to leave school until such time as they removed the arm bands.

11

On July 25, 1966, evidence was taken in the matter as follows:

PLAINTIFFS' CASE

JOHN FREDERICK TINKER, Plaintiff, testified as follows:

Direct Examination by Mr. Johnston.

My name is John Frederick Tinker, 704 Grandview; 15 years old. My parents are Leonard Edward Tinker and Mary Jean Tinker. My father is Peace Education Secretary for the American Friends Service Committee. He is a Methodist Minister, officially assigned by the Bishop to the American Friends Service Committee. I am in the 11th grade, at North High School in Des Moines, Iowa.

During the month of December, 1965, I decided to participate with several other people in a witness or demonstration of views that I have by wearing a black arm band over the holiday season. On Wednesday evening, December 15, I received a phone call from Ross Peterson, or Bruce Clark, I am not sure which one. Bruce and Ross were both members of the Liberal Religious Youth Organization at the Unitarian Church. They told me that some people had met and decided that they were going to wear arm bands during the holiday season to mourn the dead in Viet Nam and to hope for a Christmas truce that might be extended into an open ended truce. Wednesday evening they came over to my house and gave me copies of a document entitled "We Mourn" which I read and agreed with. They talked with mother and father and my sister Mary Beth and I decided to wear an arm band.

The idea of an indefinite truce was originally Robert Kennedy's and I hoped that such a truce would stop the killing and might lead to a peaceful settlement in the war. In addition to the wearing of the arm bands there was going to be a fast on New Years Eve and one other day and I did fast during those days. Also, there was a worship serv-

Document 20a. Testimony of John Tinker in *Tinker v. Des Moines*, July 25, 1966. [National Archives]

ice at the Unitarian Church on New Years Eve, but I am not sure if that was directly tied with the arm band demonstration.

I have been in several demonstrations against the war and several Civil Rights demonstrations. The subject of peace and the subject of the war in Viet Nam and the political and moral implications of it are discussed quite often in my home. These are concerns which I share with my parents and most of my brothers and sisters although I do not subscribe to all of the views of my parents.

I attend a Friends meeting and have been so attending for four years. The subjects of the conduct of war in Viet Nam and the roll of warfare and international relations and international policy are discussed at the Friends meeting quite frequently.

I had not attended any meetings concerning the wearing of arm bands prior to the one I discussed earlier on Wednesday night, but I attended most of the meetings concerning this after Wednesday.

Most of the others wore arm bands on Thursday December 16, 1965, I didn't feel that I should just wear it against the will of the principals of the high schools without even trying to talk to them first. I believe I first learned they were opposed to wearing the arm bands on Wednesday night and so I didn't wear one on Thursday because I hoped we could try to talk to the school board. Thursday evening we had a meeting with the students who had worn them Thursday and other people who were interested and the President of the school board, Mr. Niffenegger, was called, to ask him if we could meet with the school board and talk to them about the arm bands. He said no not before the next regularly scheduled meeting of the school board. That was a school day and I wore the arm band to school.

13

The first thing in the morning we had orchestra practice and I was almost late for that and was on a tight schedule, so I didn't have time to put my arm band on for that period. Nor did I have time to put it on when I went to home room, after orchestra. I put the arm band on after home room. I arrived at school around 7:30 A. M. and put the arm band on about 8:30 A. M.

The arm band was a strip of black cloth about 2 inches wide. I wore it on the left sleeve of my jacket the first part of the day and then on my shirt the second part of the day.

The instructor in the first class I wore the arm band was Mr. Thompson. I'm not sure Mr. Thompson saw me wearing the arm band. He made no comment about it. In his class we engage in group work and we were working out some sort of play and Mr. Thompson was out of the room much of the time.

I felt self-conscious about wearing the arm band. We students were talking about the play we were going to put on and some of the other students talked to me about the arm band and asked me why I was wearing it. I told them why and some of them didn't think I should do this, but they thought I should have the right to if I wanted to. This discussion took place on and off during the class period. There was no other activity about the arm band during this first class.

The next class I went to was algebra class. I got there about 10:30 and the professor was Mr. Worden. I don't believe he saw the arm band either; he made no comment about it and there was no discussion in his class at all about the arm band. I was on time for my algebra class. The next class I attended was gym during the third hour period. I wore the arm band on the way to gym class and

Document 20b. Testimony of John Tinker in *Tinker v. Des Moines*, July 25, 1966. [National Archives]

there was no discussion of that on the way to class. There was hardly no one around. I wouldn't say for sure whether there was any discussion about it in the halls on the way to the class or not. I did not wear the arm band when I had my gym clothes on, and there was no discussion of it in the gym class itself. There was some discussion before. After gym class some of the students were making fun of me for wearing it. Others, who were my friends, said they didn't want me to get in trouble. Two or three boys made remarks in the locker room that were not very friendly. This lasted for perhaps 3 or 4 minutes. They did not threaten me with any physical harm.

After gym class I had half an hour for lunch. I ate lunch in the student center with several other students with whom I eat frequently. These people warned me in a friendly manner to take the arm band off. There was one student with whom I had had a feud in the 7th grade who was making smart remarks for about 10 minutes. There were 4 or 5 people with him standing milling around. There were quite a few other students standing and milling around the lunch room. To my knowledge there were no threats to hit me or anything like that. At no time was I in fear that they might attack me or hit me in the student center because there were too many people there. I believe there were faculty members or school staff members there most of the time. No faculty member or staff member entered into any of this activity concerning the arm band in any way. A football player named Joe Thompson told the kids to leave me alone; that everybody had their own opinions.

After lunch I went to 4th period which is English with Mr. Lory. I still had the arm band on and when I arrived at the class Mr. Lory said "they are waiting for you at the office." I went down to the office; it was Mr. Wetter's office. Before arriving there I made a phone call to my

home. I think it, was my father who answered. My parents had told me if anything went wrong or I got in trouble to call. They knew that I would be wearing the arm band. Mr. Wetter is principal of North. I walked into his office and he said "I suppose you know I have to ask you take it off," and I said yes I do. He said "I don't suppose you will" or something like that and I said "no" and he said "well, I guess you know you can't wear it in schoo'". I can't remember exactly. He said it was something about a hierarchy, and that he was following orders from higher up. When I told him that I was not going to take the arm band off he told me I would have to leave school but wouldn't be suspended. He said that as soon as I took the arm band off or there was a different ruling on it that I could come back to school.

Mr. Wetter said for his own personal reasons he wanted to know why I was wearing the arm band so I told him the same thing; mourning the dead, and hoping for a Christmas truce. I guess he was in World War II and he told me about that and he made one statement that I am not sure what he meant. He said "I suppose as soon as you leave that you'll call the newspaper" and I told him that we didn't call the newspaper to begin with; that it was the school board that had made the newspapers.

My father arrived at the school and talked to Mr. Wetter for quite awhile, in my presence. We left and it was Tuesday, January 4, 1966, when I returned to school. I never received a notice of official suspension.

I had been in school in Des Moines about 8 years before this suspension and had never been suspended or been sent home before for any purpose except being sick.

I hold the same philosophies and moral beliefs now that caused me to wear the arm band and if I were to return

Document 20c. Testimony of John Tinker in *Tinker v. Des Moines*, July 25, 1966. [National Archives]

to school this fall or tomorrow I would still desire to have the right to wear an arm band to express those views.

Cross-Examination by Mr. Lovrien.

It was Wednesday night when Ross Peterson and Bruce Clark came over to my house to discuss the situation. My parents were present. Ross and Bruce told me about the arm bands and I am not sure if there was a definite decision whether or not to wear an arm band. I can't remember for sure but to my knowledge it was the first time I had heard about the idea of wearing arm bands relative to the war in Viet Nam. I hadn't made a definite decision to wear an arm band on Wednesday evening. There had been a meeting at the Eckhardt's on a Saturday night before; I believe that would have been the 11th. I couldn't say for sure whether my mother attended that meeting or not. There could have been a discussion about it in my family before Wednesday, but I can't remember.

I used a piece of black cloth. I don't know where I got it. But I ironed it neatly. Mother must have bought it, somebody bought it, but it was probably a long time prior to that. I know she didn't go out and buy black ribbon Wednesday night or whenever it was, just for the arm bands.

Thursday morning my sister Mary Beth wore a ribbon, but I didn't, and Mary Beth got sent home from school.

Also at home in December of 1965 I had a younger sister, Hope, and my younger brother, Paul. Paul is 8 and wore a black arm band to school Thursday morning. He is in second grade. Hope is 11 and in the 5th grade and I believe she wore an arm band on Thursday morning, too.

17

I suppose my mother and father have participated in most of the demonstrations against the war in Viet Nam and Civil Rights demonstrations that I have participated in.

The meeting Thursday December 16 was attended by people who had worn the arm bands on Thursday and other interested people. My sister was there, Chris Eckhardt, Chris Singer, Ross Peterson, and Bruce Clark, and others whose names I do not know. Bruce didn't wear an arm band but I am sure that Chris had worn his, and I knew on Thursday evening that he had been sent home. At the meeting we called Mr. Niffenegger and tried to talk to him. It was either Ross or Bruce one of the two who called, because they were the oldest of the group. I can't remember exactly what was said. The purpose for calling Mr. Niffenegger was that we were going to ask him if we could maybe have a discussion with him and talk to him before the school board meeting. We thought if it was brought to the school board's attention, what had happened, I really thought that they would change their decision. We recommended a meeting ahead of the regular meeting and he said no that he would not call a special meeting. He said the regular meeting would be in the next week, Tuesday, but we went on Christmas vacation Wednesday and that would have meant 3 days that we then would have been either out of school or unable to wear the arm bands.

I didn't anticipate the rule would forbid me from wearing the arm bands outside of school. I was concerned about being able to wear it to school because I didn't see anything wrong with it. I didn't think it was all that bad. In fact, I thought it was kind of good. That's why I was going to wear it. I wanted to wear it as many days in school as I could.

October 31, 1968

The President
The White House
Washington, D.C.

Mr. President:

During the past couple of years we have taken satirical
jabs at you and more than occasionally overstepped our
bounds. We disregarded the respect due the office and
the tremendous burden of running the country because of
our own emotional feelings regarding the war. We frequently disregarded the many, many good works and the
progress the country has made under your administration.

We saw the television broadcast you made last night in
behalf of the Democratic Party and Hubert Humphrey and
were quite moved by your sincerity and by the content
of the message. If the opportunity arose in this coming
election to vote for you, we would.

Often an emotional issue such as the war makes people
tend to over-react. Please accept our apology on behalf
of the Smothers Brothers Comedy Hour for our over-
reaction in some instances. Please know that we do
admire what you have done for the country and particularly your dignity in accepting the abuses of so many people.

We are now working for the election of Hubert Humphrey
and much of the enthusiasm we have for him is due to
that broadcast of yours.

Document 21a. Smothers Brothers' letter to President Johnson, October 31,
1968 (Lyndon Baines Johnson Presidential Library). [National Archives]

We just saw your message on Viet Nam and with all America,
are pleased at your determined move to halt the bombing
in an effort to achieve peace.

                              Respectfully,

                              Tom Smothers
                              Tom Smothers

                              Dick Smothers
                              Dick Smothers

DEC 18 1963

Honorable Warren G. Magnuson
Chairman, Committee on Commerce
United States Senate
Washington 25, D. C.

Dear Mr. Chairman:

This is in further reply to your request for the views of this Department with respect to S. 2345 and Amendment #335 to S. 1975, similar bills, to amend the Federal Firearms Act which regulates in certain respects the shipment of firearms in interstate and foreign commerce. This will supplement our earlier comments on S. 1975 as originally introduced, which we endorsed.

The two proposals were undoubtedly prompted in some degree by the tragic events of November 22, 1963.

Amendment #335 to S. 1975 would alter the regulatory scheme proposed in that bill in two significant respects:

1. Broaden coverage to include all firearms regardless of size, shape or description. S. 1975, as introduced, would regulate interstate retail sales of handguns, short-barrel weapons and machine guns -- essentially non-sporting weapons as distinguished from sporting types, rifles, shotguns, etc. Amendment #335 would bring the latter group within the regulation proposed.

2. The amendment would also require that the prospective purchaser's sworn statement (as to his being 18 or more years of age; not barred from acquiring under the Federal Firearms Act, i.e. not convicted or under indictment, or a fugitive from justice; and not barred by state or local law) be supplemented by a certificate of the chief law enforcement officer of the purchaser's locality attesting that the statements are true to the best of the officer's knowledge and belief.

The impact of the controls as proposed will fall primarily on those firms engaged in retail mail-order sale of firearms in interstate or foreign commerce. It will affect some of the well known, long-established firms engaged generally in the mail-order business with respect to their sales of sporting type weapons. On the other hand, direct over-the-counter retail sales, or even intrastate mail-order sales, would be left entirely to such state and local regulations as may exist or be adopted.

As indicated in our earlier comment on S. 1975, we concur in the need to strengthen controls over the distribution of firearms in interstate and foreign commerce. That a weapon is widely regarded as a sporting arm does not remove its homicidal capabilities nor insure against its use for sinister purposes, even assassination. We do not believe that the regulatory plan of S. 1975 as proposed to be amended would work undue hardship on those persons engaged in interstate retail sales nor present unreasonable obstacles to persons seeking to purchase firearms for recreational or other legitimate purposes.

Since our earlier comment on S. 1975, it has come to our attention that the bill would subject to the sworn statement and certification requirements of Section 2(1) the return shipment in interstate commerce of a repaired or modified firearm from a gunsmith to its present owner. We believe that the legitimate repair service of gunsmiths ought not to be included in the coverage of this part of the bill. We also believe that certain types of modification such as the alteration of chokes on shotguns, restocking, and changes from military to hunting sights should not be rendered more difficult. We recommend amendment of the bill to exempt these services from its provisions. However, other types of modification such as conversion to automatic fire, shortening of barrels, equipping of silencers and mufflers, and possibly the mounting of telescopic sights, might properly remain within the purview of the certification procedure.

S. 2345 would amend the present Federal Firearms Act by forbidding the sale of a firearm in interstate or foreign commerce to any person (other than a person falling within an excepted category -- police officers and the like) unless he furnishes a written statement by a local law enforcement officer. Such a statement shall cover:

1. The purchaser's stated reason for acquiring the firearm;

2. Record of indictments or convictions of purchaser (for crimes punishable by imprisonment for one year or more) from information available to certifying officer;

Document 22b. Lawrence Jones' letter to Senator Warren Magnuson about federal firearms legislation, December 18, 1963. [National Archives]

3. Information available as to whether purchaser is a fugitive;

4. Information available as to probable mental competence and stability of purchaser, and his reputation for law observance.

S. 2345 introduces the elements of probable mental competence, instability, and reputation for law observance (Sec. 2(j)(4)). While we fully agree that firearms should not go to mental incompetents, persons of unstable temperament, or habitual law breakers, the language of S. 2345 on these points, we feel, offers no objective definitions, would present serious administrative difficulties, and would invite abuse. Information as to probable mental competence might not represent sanity and competence; but might embrace unqualified statements of lay persons, reflecting personal bias, disaffection, etc. Moreover, it might include the certifying officer's own subjective opinion. The same problems will be encountered in determinations of instability and reputation for law observance.

Further, the provision of this information under the terms of the bill would impose no restriction on the sale of firearms, and thus would be ineffective. Neither S. 2345 nor the Federal Firearms Act, which it would amend, would forbid the seller to complete the sale even if the officer certifies that the prospective purchaser is probably mentally incompetent, unstable, or has a bad reputation with respect to observance of the law.

S. 2345 does not include a number of changes of the Federal Firearms Act which are proposed in S. 1975 and which have a general measure of acceptance and support. We refer, for example, to the proposal in S. 1975 to eliminate antitrust law violations and other nonviolent economic offenses, from the range of disqualifying offenses as respects acquiring firearms.

In view of the foregoing considerations, we believe that the regulatory scheme set forth in S. 1975 as proposed to be amended (amendment number 335) is preferable to that set forth in S. 2345.

Accordingly, we so recommend to your Committee.

We have been advised by the Bureau of the Budget that there would be no objection to the submission of our report to the Congress from the standpoint of the Administration's program.

Sincerely,

Lawrence Jones

Acting General Counsel

Document 22c. Lawrence Jones' letter to Senator Warren Magnuson about federal firearms legislation, December 18, 1963. [National Archives]

In The Supreme Court of the United States
October Term, 1961
no. 890 misc.
Clarence Earl Gideon, petitioner
-vs-
H.G. Cochran, Jr. Director, Division of
corrections. state of Florida respondent.

"Answer to respondent's response to petition
For writ of Certiorari."

Petitioner, Clarence Earl Gideon recieved
a copy of the response of the respondent
in the mail dated sixth day of april, 1962
Petitioner, can not make any pretense
of being able to answer the learned
attorney General of the state of Florida
because the petitioner is not a attorney
or versed in law nor does not have the
law books to copy down the decisions of
This Court. But the petitioner Knows
There is many of them. Nor would the
petitioner be allowed To do so.
according To the book of Revised
Rules of the Supreme Court of The
United States. Sent To me by Clerk of
the same Court. the response of the
respondent is out of time (Rule #24)

Under this rule the respondent has thirty days in which to make a response.

The respondent claims that a citizen can get a equal and fair trial without legal counsel.

That the constitution of the United States does not apply to the state of Florida.

Petitioner thinks that the fourteenth amend. makes this so.

Petitioner will attempt to show this court that a citizen of the state of Florida cannot get a just and fair trial without the aid of counsel

Petitioner when he wrote his petition for writ of Habeus Corpus to the Florida Supreme Court and his petition to this Court for a writ of Certiorari and this brief was and is not allowed to send out a prepared petition petitioner is required to write his petition under duress or as the attorney General states under physical restrain. If the petitioner had a attorney he could send out any kind of a petition he was so minded too. which shows he cannot have equal rights to the law unless he does have a attorney.

The same thing applies to the

Document 23b. Answer to response to petition for a writ of certiorari in *Gideon v. Wainwright*, April 19, 1962. [National Archives]

lower court. If the petitioner would of had a attorney there would not of been allowed such things as hearsay perjury or Bill of attainer against him

Petitioner claims that there was never the crime of Breaking and Entering ever committed. At that time he call on the the Federal Bureau of investagation for help at Panama City Fla. But was told They could not do nothing about it.

Respondent claims that I have no right to file petition for a writ of Habeus Corpus. take away this right to a citizen and there is nothing left

IT makes no difference how old I am or what color I am or what church I belong too if any. The question is I did not get a fair trial The question is very simple. I requested the court to appoint me attorney and the court refused. All countrys try to give there citizens a fair trial and see to it that they have counsel.

Petitioner asks of this court to disregard the response of the respondent because it was out of time and because the Attorney General did not have one of his many assistant attorney Generals to help me a citizen of the state of

Document 23c. Answer to response to petition for a writ of certiorari in *Gideon v. Wainwright*, April 19, 1962. [National Archives]

Florida To write my petition or this brief. But instead force me To write these petitions under duress

on this basis, it is respectfully urged that the petition for a Writ of certiorari shall be issue.

Clarence Earl Gideon
Petitioner

State of Florida County of Union

Petitioner Clarence Earl Gideon appearing before me a being duly sworn. affirms That The foregoing brief. That The facts or correct and True and the certificate of service That follows

Sworn and subcribed before me this 19th day of April 1962

Lawrence C Duggar
Notary of public

certificate of service

I hereby certify That a copys of the above and foregoing brief in support of writ of Certiorari has been mailed to the respondent in said cause and the attorney General State of Florida. This day of 19th Apr. 762

Clarence Earl Gideon
petitioner

Document 23d. Answer to response to petition for a writ of certiorari in *Gideon v. Wainwright*, April 19, 1962. [National Archives]

IN THE SUPREME COURT OF THE

UNITED STATES

ERNESTO A. MIRANDA,   )
)
                    Petitioner   )
)
        v.   )   AFFIDAVIT IN
)   FORMA PAUPERIS
STATE OF ARIZONA,   )
                    Respondent   )
)
....   )
_____)

        ERNESTO A. MIRANDA, being duly sworn, deposes and says:

1. I am a citizen of the United States.

2. I am the defendant-petitioner in the above-entitled action.

3. The above-entitled action came on for trial before the Superior Court of Maricopa County, Arizona, on the 20th day of June, 1963, and a verdict was returned on said date finding me guilty as charged, upon which judgment was entered.

4. An appeal was taken by petitioner from said judgment to the Supreme Court of Arizona in forma pauperis with the assistance of court appointed counsel.

5. The said court on the 22nd day of April, 1965 rendered a judgment on appeal affirming the judgment of the trial court.

6. I desire to have the decision of the Supreme Court of Arizona reviewed on certiorari by this Court, and my counsel has prepared a

petition for said writ of certiorari which
it is desired to file forthwith in the office of the Clerk of the Supreme Court.

7. I believe that fundamental constitutional
error has been committed by the trial court
and the Supreme Court of Arizona, and this
petition is filed in good faith.

8. Because of my poverty, I am unable to pay
the costs of said petition for writ of
certiorari or to print the record therein
or to give security for the same.

9. This affidavit is made for the purpose of
availing myself of the rights and privileges
in such case provided by Sec. 1915 of Title
28 of the United States Code.

Ernesto A. Miranda
Ernesto A. Miranda

STATE OF ARIZONA   )
) ss.
COUNTY OF PINAL   )

      Subscribed and sworn to before me at Florence,
Arizona, this 3rd day of July, 1965.

Notary Public
Notary Public

My Commission Expires:
My Commission Expires June 1, 1968

-2-

THE GRAND JURORS SELECTED, CHOSEN, AND SWORN FOR THE
COUNTY OF **CHATHAM**, TO-WIT:

1	Walter A. Fulmer	Foreman	
2	Armand D. Wells	13	Mary E. Heidt
3	W. ClaggettGilbert, Jr.	14	Thomas C. Bordeaux
4	Eugene G. Hardy	15	James A. Eason
5	Ralph E. Kennickell	16	Frank J. Finocchiaro
6	Richard Singleton	17	Eros K. Bell
7	Charles L. Stewart	18	Dwight L. Bliss, Sr.
8	William L. Hopkins, Jr.	19	Jake Fine, Jr.
9	William D. Mathews	20	Fred H. Quante
10	Glenn C. Kimble	21	Hugh H. Jackson, Jr.
11	James R. Fisher	22	David A. Byck, III
12	J. Fleming Bel	23	Frederick J. Hart, Jr.

in the name and behalf of the citizens of Georgia, charge and accuse

WILLIAM HENRY FURMAN

of the county and State aforesaid, with the offense of   MURDER

for that the said   Defendant

in the County of Chatham and State of Georgia aforesaid, on the   11th

day of   August   in the year of our Lord one thousand nine hundred and

sixty -seven , with force and arms,   Did unlawfully and with malice afore-

thought kill and murder William J. Micke, by shooting the said

William J. Micke with a pistol, contrary to the laws of the State of

Georgia, the good order, peace and dignity thereof.

_____

SOLICITOR GENERAL, EASTERN JUDICIAL
CIRCUIT OF GEORGIA.

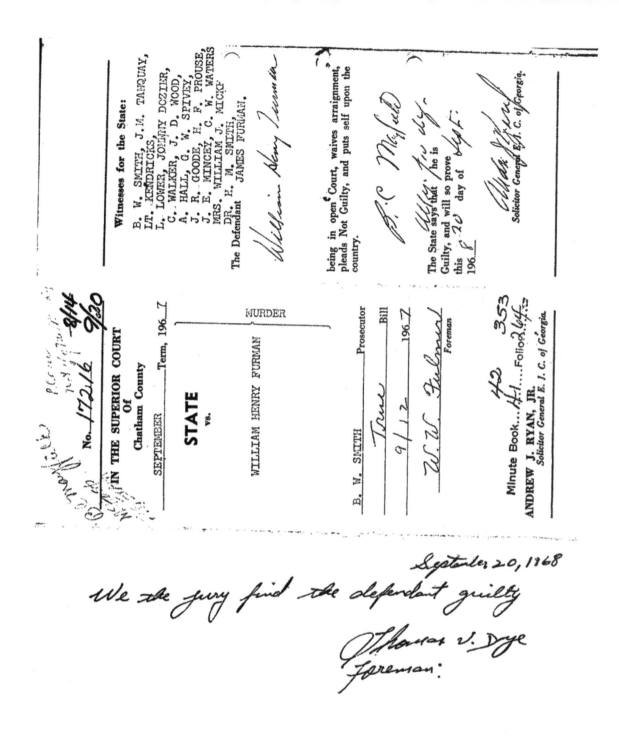

Document 25b. Selections from the transcript of record of *Furman v. Georgia*, August 11, 1967, and September 20, 1968. [National Archives]

IN THE SUPERIOR COURT OF CHATHAM COUNTY, GEORGIA

EASTERN JUDICIAL CIRCUIT

SEPTEMBER 1968 TERM

INDICTMENT NO. 17216

CHARGE: MURDER

STATE OF GEORGIA

VS

WILLIAM HENRY FURMAN

PLEA: OF NOT GUILTY

VERDICT: GUILTY

SENTENCE OF THE COURT

The above defendant, _____ William Henry Furman _____ having on _____ September 20, 1968 _____ at the present Term of Court, been convicted in the Superior Court of Chatham County, Georgia, of the offense of murder, a capital crime, without recommendation,

IT IS THEREFORE CONSIDERED, ORDERED AND ADJUDGED that the said

_____ William Henry Furman _____

be delivered to the Director of Corrections for electrocution at such penal institution as may be designated by said Director, and the said defendant shall, on _____ November 8, 1968 _____, be put to death by electrocution in the manner provided by law.

IN OPEN COURT, this _____ September 20, 1968 _____.

_____ Dunbar Harrison _____
Judge Superior Court
Eastern Judicial Circuit of Georgia

Andrew J. Ryan, Jr.
Solicitor General

B. Clarence Mayfield
Attorney for Defendant

6/7/65

16

Document 25c. Selections from the transcript of record of *Furman v. Georgia*, August 11, 1967, and September 20, 1968. [National Archives]

LEGISLATIVE NOTICE

Editor, Jody Baldwin

Notice # 101
February 1, 1984

U.S. SENATE REPUBLICAN POLICY COMMITTEE
John Tower, Chairman

Calendar 356

S. 1765: ESTABLISHING CONSTITUTIONAL PROCEDURES FOR IMPOSITION OF CAPITAL PUNISHMENT

REPORTED: August 4 (legis. day, August 1), 1983; Judiciary (S. Rept. 98-251)

CAPSULE VERSION

PURPOSE: Amend U.S. Criminal Code to: (1) Provide **death penalty for murder, treason, espionage, or killing (or attempting to kill) President** under specified circumstances IF it is determined death sentence is justified in post-verdict sentencing hearing where mitigating and aggravating factors are considered; (2) specify statutory **mitigating and aggravating factors** to be considered by jury or judge in determining justification for death penalty; (3) set forth procedures for **special post-verdict sentencing hearing;** (4) **require court to impose sentence of death** IF jury or judge return finding death penalty is justified; (5) provide rules applicable to **appeals from imposition of death** sentence; (6) reduce scope of availability of death penalty for espionage, allowing death penalty for peacetime espionage ONLY where it concerns major military matters directly affecting **national defense;** (7) provide death penalty for **first-degree murder of foreign, official, official U.S. guest, or an internationally protected person;** (8) provide death penalty for **"lifer" in Federal prison who murders anyone in prison** (guard, another prisoner, visitor, etc.); (9) provide death penalty where **death results from kidnapping;** (10) **eliminate death penalty** as authorized punishment **for rape within special maritime and territorial jurisdiction of U.S.;** (11) restrict use of death penalty in **bank robberies** and incidental crimes to those cases where death results, making life imprisonment an alternative penalty; and (12) make bill's sentencing procedures applicable to first-degree murder in U.S. special maritime and territorial jurisdiction and **whenever death occurs as** result of (a) damage to aircraft or motor vehicles, (b) transporting explosive in interstate commerce to injure persons or property, (c) destruction of government property by explosive, (d) malicious destruction by explosives of property used in interstate commerce, (e) mailing of injurious articles, (f) wrecking of trains, and (g) aircraft piracy (deleting mandatory death penalty for all aircraft piracy offenses).

(For details, see below.)

BACKGROUND: In 1972, the U.S. Supreme Court in *Furman v. Georgia* in effect made death penalty provisions in Federal and State laws inoperative by holding that, because of the unlimited discretion given to the judge and jury under then-existing statutes, the death penalty had come to be imposed so arbitrarily and capriciously as to constitute cruel and unusual punishment in violation of 8th Amendment. At the time of that decision, Federal law authorized death penalty for 6 categories of offenses -- espionage, treason, first-degree murder, felony-murder, rape, and kidnapping (when victim was not freed unharmed and when kidnapping was committed during bank robbery).

The challenge set by the Court for Congress (and State legislatures) was not so much one of specifying those offenses for which death penalty should be authorized (since Federal law already did this), but one of designing a procedure and establishing criteria for imposition of death penalty which would bring the "arbitrary and capricious" result flowing from unfettered discretion within constitutionally tolerable bounds. In response to *Furman,* 35 State legislatures enacted new laws attempting to meet the objections of the Supreme Court by removing the imposition of death penalty from unguided discretion of the judge and jury. The Congress enacted anti-hijacking legislation providing for procedures for imposition of death penalty for aircraft hijacking where death results, but failed to act on general legislation to cover Federal murder, treason, and espionage.

As result of *Furman*, Senators Hruska and McClellan introduced a bill in the 93d Congress (March 27, 1973) to provide constitutional procedures and criteria for imposing death penalty for most Federal offenses then authorizing death penalty. The bill, S. 1401, passed the Senate on March 13, 1974, by vote of 54 to 33, but the House did not act on it. Thereafter, the Congress delayed acting on other bills until decisions were rendered in a group of post-*Furman* cases pending before Supreme Court. In 1976 (94th Congress) the court decided this group of landmark death penalty cases by holding death penalty was constitutional when imposed under certain procedures and criteria which guarded against unfettered discretion (condemned in *Furman*), but which retained important flexibility to consider aggravating and mitigating factors of each case. Mandatory death penalty laws were struck down (*Roberts v. Louisiana*).

In the 95th Congress, a bill was introduced and was the subject of hearings which reflected the latest decisions by the Supreme Court, but it was never reported by the full Senate Judiciary Committee; in the 96th Congress, a bill was reported by that Committee to the full Senate to meet constitutional requirements of guided discretion based on rational criteria (similar to other bills), but the Senate did not act on it. S. 114, introduced by Senators DeConcini and Thurmond on January 15, 1981 (97th Congress), was amended by Judiciary and reported on July 1, 1981, but was not taken up on Senate floor. In this Congress, 2 bills, S. 538 and S. 829, contained provisions on capital punishment; further hearings were held; and S. 1765 was introduced by Senator Thurmond on August 4, 1983, immediately referred to and reported by Judiciary, and placed on Senate Calendar. Its provisions were NOT included in the crime package, S. 1762, because of the controversy surrounding the death penalty.

ISSUES: **Capital Punishment as Matter of Legislative Policy** -- Despite Supreme Court's explicit approval of death penalty as appropriate sanction under 8th Amendment, committee felt compelled to justify its use under particular circumstances provided in bill. Retention of capital punishment has two underlying beliefs: (1) Primary responsibility of society is protection of its members to live in peace and safety; and (2) purpose of criminal law is to promote respect for lives and property of others.

Deterrence -- Question of deterrent effect of capital punishment has been one point most debated by those favoring abolition of death penalty and those desiring its retention. While several studies have been conducted purporting to show absence of any correlation between death penalty and number of capital crimes committed in a particular jurisdiction, the statistical evidence is diminished by its unreliability, and, at best, available data is inconclusive. (Those who are deterred by threat of death penalty and do not commit murder are NOT included in the statistical data.) In absence of reliable statistical evidence, great weight must be put on experience of those most frequently called on to deal with murderers and potential murderers and are thus in best position to judge effectiveness of remedy -- our law enforcement officials. Vast majority of these officials continue to favor retention of death penalty as deterrent to violent crime. The issue, for committee's purposes, was definitely resolved by the Supreme Court in *Gregg v. Georgia* when it concluded it was appropriate for a legislature to consider deterrence as a justification for imposition of death penalty.

Incapacitation -- Incapacitating effect of capital punishment is clear -- those who suffer this penalty are unable to commit similar crimes again. Question then becomes one of necessity. Is death penalty necessary to adequately protect society from possible actions of those who have already committed capital crimes? Committee believes it is necessary in some circumstances. In some cases, imprisonment is simply not sufficient safeguard against future actions of criminals. Some criminals are incorrigibly anti-social, will remain potentially dangerous for the rest of their lives, and will present threat to other inmates, guards, etc., even if they are imprisoned for life. Committee's desire is NOT to see capital punishment used as alternative to rehabilitation, but committee recognizes still greater attempts must be made to enable prison system to actually restore productive and useful individuals to society.

Retribution -- Committee also finds that capital punishment serves legitimate function of retribution. Distinct from concept of revenge ("eye for an eye" mentality), it is through retribution that society expresses its outrage and sense of revulsion toward those who undermine foundations of civilized society by contravening its laws. It reflects fact criminals have not simply inflicted injury upon discrete individuals; they have also weakened often tenuous bonds that hold communities together. Committee believes feelings and demands of the community rightly and justly warrant imposition of capital punishment under some circumstances. Murder does not simply differ in magnitude from extortion or burglary or property destruction; it differs in kind -- and its punishment should also differ in kind. Its punishment must acknowledge inviolability and dignity of innocent human life. But committee concludes it is not enough to proclaim sanctity and importance of innocent life. Innocent life must be, and can only be, secured by a society that is willing to impose its highest penalty upon those who threaten such life.

Possibility of Error -- Argument often used in favor of abolishing death penalty concerns, dangers of executing the innocent which is, obviously, an irremediable mistake. Then, argument is made that, since cost of such a mistake is so great, risk of imposing death penalty at all is unacceptable. Committee finds such argument without great weight, particularly in light of procedural safeguards mandated by Supreme Court in recent years for criminal defendants. Indeed, committee is aware of NO case where an innocent man has been put to death. While this possibility does continue to exist because of man's fallible nature, committee feels minimal risk is justified by protection afforded society by death penalty.

Public Opinion -- In arriving at decision to support death penalty, committee gave considerable weight to public opinion. Contrary to frequently asserted statement that there is growing public opposition to capital punishment, examination of public opinion polls over last 10 years shows remarkable rise in Americans favoring death penalty -- from 49 percent in 1971 to its highest point after attempt on President Reagan's life in 1981 when 66 percent favored death penalty for murder convictions.

PURPOSE: To amend U.S. Criminal Code to meet constitutional requirements enunciated by Supreme Court on **capital punishment**, as follows:

Sec. 1: Amend U.S. Criminal Code to: (1) **Require defendant found guilty of homicide, treason, espionage, or killing (or attempting to kill) President be sentenced to death IF**, after consideration of mitigating and aggravating factors, it is determined death sentence is justified in **post-verdict sentencing hearing**; (2) provide defendant, to be subject to **death penalty for homicide,** must have intentionally killed victim, intentionally inflicted serious bodily injury which resulted in death of victim, or intentionally participated in an act he knew (or reasonably should have known) would create grave risk of death to someone other than person participating in offense and victim died as direct result thereof; (3) provide **death penalty for ATTEMPTS to kill President ONLY IF** bodily injury resulted to the President or he came dangerously close to death; (4) set forth **four statutory mitigating factors** to be considered by jury or judge in determining whether to impose sentence of death -- defendant (a) was under 18 at time of crime, (b) had significantly impaired mental capacity (but not so impaired as to constitute a defense), (c) was under unusual and substantial duress (but not enough to constitute a defense), and (d) was an accomplice whose participation in offense was relatively minor; (5) state jury or judge may consider whether **other mitigating factors exist**; (6) set forth **statutory aggravating factors to be considered for treason and espionage** -- defendant (a) convicted of another offense involving espionage or treason for which sentence of either life imprisonment or death was authorized by law, (b) knowingly created grave risk of substantial danger to national security, or (c) knowingly created grave risk of death to another person; (7) set forth **statutory aggravating factors** to be considered for **homicide or attempting to kill the President** -- defendant (a) was attempting to commit, or fleeing from, certain dangerous crimes (escape from penal custody, espionage, serious explosive offenses, murder by prisoner serving life sentence, kidnapping, treason, and aircraft hijacking) AND death or fatal injury occurred to another, (b) had previously been convicted of 2 or more Federal or State offenses resulting in death and for which life imprisonment or death was authorized by law, (c) had previously been convicted of 2 or more Federal or State offenses (committed on different occasions) bearing penalty of over 1 year imprisonment and involving serious bodily injury to another, (d) knowingly created grave risk of death to one or more persons in addition to victim of offense, (e) committed offense in especially heinous, cruel, or depraved manner, (f) procured commission of offense by payment, (g) committed offense for pay, (h) committed offense after substantial planning and premeditation to cause another's death or committed an act of terrorism, or (i) committed offense against one of certain designated public officials [President, President-elect, Vice President, Vice President-elect, Vice President-designate, other officer next in order of succession to being President if there is no Vice President; head of state, etc., of foreign nation; certain foreign officials in U.S. on official business; or Federal public servant -- judge, law enforcement officer, or employee of U.S. penal/correctional system -- while he is engaged in official duties, because of such duties, or because of his official position]; (8) IF government believes circumstances of above specified offenses justify death penalty, require government to give notice of such to defendant, setting forth aggravating factors it proposes to prove to justify death sentence; (9) provide such notice must be filed with court and served on defendant a reasonable time before trial, before acceptance by court of defendant's guilty plea, or whenever court may permit thereafter upon showing of good cause; (10) require judge, in cases where government has filed such notice and defendant was found guilty of offense punishable by death, to conduct separate sentencing hearing to determine punishment to be imposed; (11) require such hearing be conducted (a) before jury which determined defendant's guilt, or (b) before new jury impaneled for hearing if original jury was discharged for good cause (or if defendant was convicted upon guilty plea or by court sitting without a jury), or (c) before court alone IF defendant so moves and government approves; (12) require such jury consist of 12 members UNLESS parties stipulate before conclusion of hearing it shall consist of fewer and court approves; (13) allow any information relevant to sentence to be presented at hearing, including information on mitigating or aggravating factors (i.e., trial transcripts and exhibits; other information regardless of its admissibility under rules of evidence); (14) provide that sentencing decision shall be made on basis of information received during sentencing hearing, with both attorneys allowed to rebut such information and with special finding required to be returned which identifies whether any statutory mitigating or aggravating factors were found; (15) IF aggravating factors are found to exist, jury (or court) must then decide whether they sufficiently outweigh all mitigating factors found to exist in order to justify sentence of death, etc.; (16) require jury be instructed in any sentencing hearing NOT to consider race, color, national origin, creed, or sex of defendant; (17) require court to impose death sentence IF jury (or judge) returns finding death penalty is justified; (18) IF death sentence is NOT found to be justified, allow court to impose any other authorized sentence, allowing life imprisonment without parole to be imposed for a conviction IF maximum term of imprisonment for such offense is life imprisonment; (19) provide sentence of death imposed under bill's provisions will be subject to review by court of appeals upon appeal by defendant, with notice of appeal required to be filed within time specified for filing of such appeals (thereby allowing consolidation of appeals for convictions with appeals from sentences for same crimes) and requiring that review of appeals in capital cases take precedence over all other appeals; (20) require appeals court to consider entire record in case, procedures employed in sentencing hearing, and findings as to presence of aggravating and mitigating factors; (21) require appeals court to affirm sentence IF it finds death sentence was NOT imposed under influence of passion, prejudice, or other arbitrary factor AND information supports jury's or court's special findings, but, IN ALL OTHER CASES, require appeals court to remand case for reconsideration, with written reasons for decision in either instance; (22) require person sentenced to death under bill's provisions be committed to Attorney General's custody pending completion of appeal and review process, with person turned over to custody of U.S. Marshals when sentence is to be implemented; (23) allow State facilities to be hired to carry out death sentences; and (24) prohibit sentence of death from being carried out on woman who is pregnant.

Sec. 2:   Amend U.S. Criminal Code to make sentencing procedure applicable to violations dealing with aircraft and motor vehicles resulting in death.

Sec. 3:   Amend U.S. Criminal Code to reduce scope of death penalty for espionage so that death is authorized sentence for peacetime espionage ONLY where it concerns certain major military matters directly affecting national defense (i.e., nuclear weaponry, military spacecraft or satellites, early warning systems or other defense or retaliation against large-scale attack, war plans, communications intelligence or cryptographic information, or any other major weapons system or major element of defense strategy).

Sec. 4:   Amend U.S. Criminal Code to make sentencing procedure applicable to violations dealing with transportation of explosives in interstate commerce with knowledge or intent to use them to injure persons or property where death results.

Sec. 5:   Amend U.S. Criminal Code to make sentencing procedure applicable to violations dealing with destruction of Government or Government-related property by explosives where death results.

Sec. 6:   Amend U.S. Criminal Code to make sentencing procedure applicable to violations dealing with malicious destruction by explosives of property used in interstate commerce where death results.

Sec. 7:   Amend U.S. Criminal Code to make sentencing procedure applicable to offense of first-degree murder committed in special maritime and territorial jurisdiction of U.S.

Sec. 8:   Amend U.S. Criminal Code (a) to increase maximum penalty for first-degree murder of foreign official or official guest while in U.S. to include death and (b) to make sentencing procedure applicable to such offense.

Sec. 9:   Amend U.S. Criminal Code to create new Federal offense under which a Federal prisoner serving a life term who murders anyone in prison (guard, visitor, another prisoner) can be punished either by death or by term of life imprisonment without parole.

Sec. 10:   Amend U.S. Criminal Code (a) to impose death penalty where death results from kidnapping and (b) to make sentencing procedure applicable to such offense.

Sec. 11:   Amend U.S. Criminal Code to make sentencing procedure applicable to violations dealing with mailing of injurious articles where death results.

Sec. 12:   Amend U.S. Criminal Code (a) to impose death penalty for attempt to kill the President IF attempt results in his bodily injury or otherwise comes dangerously close to killing him, and (b) to make sentencing procedure applicable to such offense.

Sec. 13:   Amend U.S. Criminal Code to make sentencing procedure applicable to violations dealing with wrecking of trains where death results.

Sec. 14:   Amend U.S. Criminal Code to delete death penalty as authorized punishment for rape within special maritime and territorial jurisdiction of U.S.

Sec. 15:   Amend U.S. Criminal Code to restrict death penalty for violations concerning bank robbery and incidental crimes to those cases where death results, providing life imprisonment as alternative penalty in such cases.

Sec. 16:   Amend U.S. Criminal Code (a) to make sentencing procedure applicable to violations dealing with aircraft piracy where death results from commission (or attempted commission) of offense, but (b) to repeal present law punishing any aircraft piracy with death.

Sec. 17:   Provide that special procedures for imposition of death penalty and for appellate review of that sentence shall NOT apply to prosecutions under Uniform Code of Military Justice.

COST: Not likely to be significant.

REGULATORY IMPACT: None.

MINORITY VIEWS: Senators Kennedy, Metzenbaum, and Leahy. While unchecked growth of violent crime has become source of fear and alarm for all people, which they share, do NOT believe solution rests with death penalty. Believe death penalty is WRONG: (1) As matter of public policy because (a) capital punishment places incredible strains on criminal justice system, far outweighing any marginal benefit that arguably is gained, (b) support of capital punishment is quick, shorthand method for appearing to be tough on crime and there is no evidence it will deter violent crime, (c) legislation does little to alleviate fears caused by increase in number of robberies, muggings, burglaries, and assaults, (d) imposition of death penalty leaves no room for mistakes, and (e) those who have been sentenced to death overwhelmingly come from the poor and minorities; (2) as matter of principle because (a) death penalty is harshest punishment which can be inflicted and (b) act of premeditated execution is itself a debasing denial of sanctity of life; and (3) as matter of constitutional law because this bill (a) permits imposition of death penalty for crimes where death does not result (treason and espionage, for instance), (b) permits jury to disagree as to which aggravating factor they have relied on so long as they all agree some aggravating factor is present (thereby allowing death penalty to be imposed although majority of jurors may not have agreed on any aggravating factor), and (c) does NOT include third determination required by judge in appellate review -- that sentence of death is not excessive, considering both crime and defendant (thereby eliminating constitutionally mandated requirement, in *Coker v. Georgia*, that appellate court must look at death penalty sentence to determine whether it is out of proportion to crime's severity). Majority has NOT made persuasive case that death penalty will deter violent crime or meet constitutional requirements of due process of law and equal protection of the laws.

— — —

ADMINISTRATION POSITION: The Administration supports enactment of S. 1765.

Sixty-eighth Congress of the United States of America;

At the First Session,

Begun and held at the City of Washington on Monday, the third day of December, one thousand nine hundred and twenty-three.

JOINT RESOLUTION

Proposing an amendment to the Constitution of the United States.

Resolved by the Senate and House of Representatives of the United States of America in Congress assembled (two-thirds of each House concurring therein), That the following article is proposed as an amendment to the Constitution of the United States, which, when ratified by the legislatures of three-fourths of the several States, shall be valid to all intents and purposes as a part of the Constitution:

"ARTICLE —

"SECTION 1. The Congress shall have power to limit, regulate, and prohibit the labor of persons under eighteen years of age.

"SEC. 2. The power of the several States is unimpaired by this article except that the operation of State laws shall be suspended to the extent necessary to give effect to legislation enacted by the Congress."

F H GILLETT
Speaker of the House of Representatives.

ALBERT B. CUMMINS
President pro tempore of the Senate.

I certify that this Joint Resolution originated in the House of Representatives.

WM TYLER PAGE
Clerk.

Document 27. H. J. Res. (House joint resolution) 184, proposing an amendment to control child labor, December 3, 1923. [National Archives]

CHILD HEALTH DAY, 1956

- - - - - - - -

BY THE PRESIDENT OF THE UNITED STATES OF AMERICA

A PROCLAMATION

WHEREAS the Congress, by a joint resolution of May 18, 1928 (45 Stat. 617), has authorized and requested the President of the United States to issue annually a proclamation setting apart May 1 as Child Health Day; and

WHEREAS Child Health Day provides us with an occasion for dedicating ourselves anew to the task of promoting the spiritual, emotional, and physical well-being of children; and

WHEREAS it is fitting that we foster the health and welfare of our children in order that they may grow into responsible citizens and may contribute to the peace and productivity of the world; and

WHEREAS Child Health Day is an appropriate time for the citizens of the United States to observe also a Universal Children's Day, and to salute the work which the United Nations Children's Fund, the World Health Organization, and the Food and Agriculture Organization are doing, through the United Nations, to build better health for children:

NOW, THEREFORE, I, DWIGHT D. EISENHOWER, President of the United States of America, do hereby designate Tuesday, the first day of May 1956, as Child Health Day, and I invite all citizens to unite in observances that will emphasize the importance of abundant health for all children.

IN WITNESS WHEREOF, I have hereunto set my hand and caused the Seal of the United States of America to be affixed.

DONE at the City of Washington this *Second* day of *April* in the year of our Lord nineteen hundred and fifty-six, and of the Independence of the United States of America the one hundred and eightieth.

Dwight Eisenhower

By the President

Secretary of State

Document 28b. Proclamation by President Eisenhower of Child Health Day, April 2, 1956. [National Archives]

H. R. 13247

Eighty-fifth Congress of the United States of America

AT THE SECOND SESSION

Begun and held at the City of Washington on Tuesday, the seventh day of January, one thousand nine hundred and fifty-eight

An Act

To strengthen the national defense and to encourage and assist in the expansion and improvement of educational programs to meet critical national needs; and for other purposes.

Be it enacted by the Senate and House of Representatives of the United States of America in Congress assembled, That this Act, divided into titles and sections according to the following table of contents, may be cited as the "National Defense Education Act of 1958".

TABLE OF CONTENTS

Document 29a. National Defense Education Act, September 2, 1958. [National Archives]

ALLOTMENTS TO TERRITORIES AND POSSESSIONS

SEC. 1008. The amounts reserved by the Commissioner under sections 302 and 502 shall be allotted by the Commissioner among Alaska, Hawaii, Puerto Rico, the Canal Zone, Guam, and the Virgin Islands, according to their respective needs for the type of assistance furnished under the part or title in which the section appears.

IMPROVEMENT OF STATISTICAL SERVICES OF STATE EDUCATIONAL AGENCIES

SEC. 1009. (a) For the purpose of assisting the States to improve and strengthen the adequacy and reliability of educational statistics provided by State and local reports and records and the methods and techniques for collecting and processing educational data and disseminating information about the condition and progress of education in the States, there are hereby authorized to be appropriated for the fiscal year ending June 30, 1959, and each of the three succeeding fiscal years, for grants to States under this section, such sums as the Congress may determine.

(b) Grants under this section by the Commissioner shall be equal to one-half of the cost of State educational agency programs to carry out the purposes of this section, including (1) improving the collection, analysis, and reporting of statistical data supplied by local educational units, (2) the development of accounting and reporting manuals to serve as guides for local educational units, (3) the conduct of conferences and training for personnel of local educational units and of periodic reviews and evaluation of the program for records and reports, (4) improving methods for obtaining, from other State agencies within the State, educational data not collected by the State educational agency, or (5) expediting the processing and reporting of statistical data through installation and operation of mechanical equipment. The total of the payments to any State under this section for any fiscal year may not exceed $50,000.

(c) Payments with respect to any program of a State educational agency under this section may be made (1) only to the extent it is a new program or an addition to or expansion of an existing program, and (2) only if the State plan approved under subsection (d) includes such program.

(d) The Commissioner shall approve any State plan for purposes of this section if such plan meets the requirements of section 1004 (a) and sets forth the programs proposed to be carried out under the plan and the general policies to be followed in doing so.

Speaker of the House of Representatives.

Vice President of the United States and
President of the Senate.

APPROVED

SEP 2 1958

48

Exhibit 4

IN THE SUPERIOR COURT OF THE STATE OF ARIZONA

IN AND FOR THE COUNTY OF GILA

HAVING AND EXERCISING JURISDICTION IN JUVENILE MATTERS

COMMITMENT TO THE STATE

INDUSTRIAL SCHOOL, No. 2379

In the Matter of

GERALD FRANCIS GAULT

a Delinquent Minor

A Petition having been heretofore filed by Charles D. Flagg, Probation Officer for the County of Gila, State of Arizona, charging the aforesaid minor with being a delinquent child within the meaning of the Statutes of the State of Arizona applicable thereto;

Now, this 15th day of June, 1964, said matter coming on regularly to be heard before the Judge of the said Superior Court of said County of Gila, in Chambers, and after a full hearing and due deliberation the Court finds that said minor is a delinquent child, and that said minor is of the age of 15 years.

And the Court finds that the said child's own good and the best interests of the State require that he be committed to the State Industrial School for the period of his minority, unless sooner discharged by due process of law.

49

A certified copy of this Order shall be a warrant for the Probation Officer of Gila County to deliver the said child to said Industrial School, and for the authorities of said Industrial School to receive and keep said child as herein ordered and provided.

DATED AT GLOBE, ARIZONA, this 15th day of June, 1964.

/s/ ROBERT E. McGHEE

Robert E. McGhee, *Judge of the Superior Court*

Document 30. Commitment order to state industrial school from the case of *in re Gault,* June 15, 1964. [National Archives]

ALAMO HEIGHTS STUDENT COUNCIL

6900 BROADWAY

SAN ANTONIO, TEXAS 78209

Student Rights Committee

Dear Justice Douglas,

I would like to request whatever information you may have on the case of <u>Goss v. Lopez</u>. All that I know about the case is that it involves a question of student rights and that an "amicus curiae" brief should be before the Supreme Court at the moment.

I am researching student rights in the hope of developing an exact statement of those rights, and I am in great need of background material. I would appreciate any help you can offer, perhaps in the way of suggesting what other decisions I could look into.

Thank you for your assistance.

Sincerely,
Ralph V. Evans
Chairman, Bills Subcommittee

Document 31. Ralph Evans' letter to Justice Douglas about *Goss v. Lopez*, 1974. [National Archives]

EXECUTIVE ORDER

- - - - - - -

AUTHORIZING THE SECRETARY OF WAR TO PRESCRIBE MILITARY AREAS

WHEREAS the successful prosecution of the war requires every possible protection against espionage and against sabotage to national-defense material, national-defense premises, and national-defense utilities as defined in Section 4, Act of April 20, 1918, 40 Stat. 533, as amended by the Act of November 30, 1940, 54 Stat. 1220, and the Act of August 21, 1941, 55 Stat. 655 (U. S. C., Title 50, Sec. 104):

NOW, THEREFORE, by virtue of the authority vested in me as President of the United States, and Commander in Chief of the Army and Navy, I hereby authorize and direct the Secretary of War, and the Military Commanders whom he may from time to time designate, whenever he or any designated Commander deems such action necessary or desirable, to prescribe military areas in such places and of such extent as he or the appropriate Military Commander may determine, from which any or all persons may be excluded, and with respect to which, the right of any person to enter, remain in, or leave shall be subject to whatever restrictions the Secretary of War or the appropriate Military

Commander may impose in his discretion. The Secretary of War is hereby authorized to provide for residents of any such area who are excluded therefrom, such transportation, food, shelter, and other accommodations as may be necessary, in the judgment of the Secretary of War or the said Military Commander, and until other arrangements are made, to accomplish the purpose of this order. The designation of military areas in any region or locality shall supersede designations of prohibited and restricted areas by the Attorney General under the Proclamations of December 7 and 8, 1941, and shall supersede the responsibility and authority of the Attorney General under the said Proclamations in respect of such prohibited and restricted areas.

I hereby further authorize and direct the Secretary of War and the said Military Commanders to take such other steps as he or the appropriate Military Commander may deem advisable to enforce compliance with the restrictions applicable to each Military area hereinabove authorized to be designated, including the use of Federal troops and other Federal Agencies, with authority to accept assistance of state and local agencies.

I hereby further authorize and direct all Executive Departments, independent establishments and other Federal Agencies, to assist the Secretary of War or the said Military Commanders in carrying out this Executive Order, including the furnishing of medical aid, hospitalization, food, clothing, transportation, use of land, shelter, and other supplies, equipment, utilities, facilities, and services.

This order shall not be construed as modifying or limiting in any way the authority heretofore granted under Executive Order No. 8972, dated December 12, 1941, nor shall it be construed as limiting or modifying the duty and responsibility of the Federal Bureau of Investigation, with respect to the investigation of alleged acts of sabotage or the duty and responsibility of the Attorney General and the Department of Justice under the Proclamations of December 7 and 8, 1941, prescribing regulations for the conduct and control of alien enemies, except as such duty and responsibility is superseded by the designation of military areas hereunder.

THE WHITE HOUSE,

February 19, 1942.

Franklin D. Roosevelt

Document 32c. Executive Order No. 9066, February 19, 1942. [National Archives]

Seventy-seventh Congress of the United States of America;

At the Second Session

Begun and held at the City of Washington on Monday, the fifth
day of January, one thousand nine hundred and forty-two

AN ACT

To provide a penalty for violation of restrictions or orders with
respect to persons entering, remaining in, leaving, or committing
any act in military areas or zones.

*Be it enacted by the Senate and House of Representatives of the
United States of America in Congress assembled,* That whoever shall
enter, remain in, leave, or commit any act in any military area or
military zone prescribed, under the authority of an Executive order
of the President, by the Secretary of War, or by any military commander designated by the Secretary of War, contrary to the restrictions applicable to any such area or zone or contrary to the order of
the Secretary of War or any such military commander, shall, if it
appears that he knew or should have known of the existence and
extent of the restrictions or order and that his act was in violation
thereof, be guilty of a misdemeanor and upon conviction shall be
liable to a fine of not to exceed $5,000 or to imprisonment for not
more than one year, or both, for each offense.

Speaker of the House of Representatives.

Vice President of the United States and
President of the Senate.

President of the Senate pro tempore.

Approved
Mar 21 1942

Document 33. Public Law 503, March 21, 1942. [National Archives]

RELOCATION PROJECT SITES

CENTRAL UTAH: CAPACITY: 10,000
ABRAHAM, MILLARD COUNTY, UTAH
140 MILES SOUTHWEST OF SALT LAKE CITY
4 MILES NORTHWEST OF DELTA

COLORADO RIVER: CAPACITY: 20,000
POSTON, YUMA COUNTY, ARIZONA
12 MILES SOUTH OF PARKER
HALFWAY BETWEEN NEEDLES AND YUMA

GILA RIVER: CAPACITY 15,000
SACATON, PINAL COUNTY, ARIZONA
50 MILES SOUTH OF PHOENIX
3 MILES WEST OF SACATON

GRANADA: CAPACITY: 8,000
GRANADA, PROWERS COUNTY, COLORADO
140 MILES EAST OF PUEBLO
1¼ MILES SOUTHWEST OF GRANADA

HEART MOUNTAIN: CAPACITY: 11,000
VOCATION, PARK COUNTY, WYOMING
13 MILES NORTHEAST OF CODY
8 MILES SOUTH OF RALSTON

JEROME: CAPACITY: 10,000
JEROME, CHICOT AND DREW COS, ARKANSAS
30 MILES SOUTHWEST OF ARKANSAS CITY
8 MILES SOUTH OF DERMOTT

MANZANAR: CAPACITY: 10,000
MANZANAR, INYO COUNTY, CALIFORNIA
225 MILES NORTH OF LOS ANGELES
5 MILES SOUTH OF INDEPENDENCE

MINIDOKA: CAPACITY: 10,000
GOODING, JEROME COUNTY, IDAHO
25 MILES NORTHEAST OF TWIN FALLS
8 MILES NORTH OF EDEN

ROHWER: CAPACITY: 10,000
ROHWER, DESHA COUNTY, ARKANSAS
25 MILES NORTHWEST OF ARKANSAS CITY
8 MILES SOUTH OF WATSON

TULE LAKE: CAPACITY: 16,000
NEWELL, MODOC COUNTY, CALIFORNIA
35 MILES SOUTHEAST OF KLAMATH FALLS
2 MILES SOUTH OF STRONGHOLD

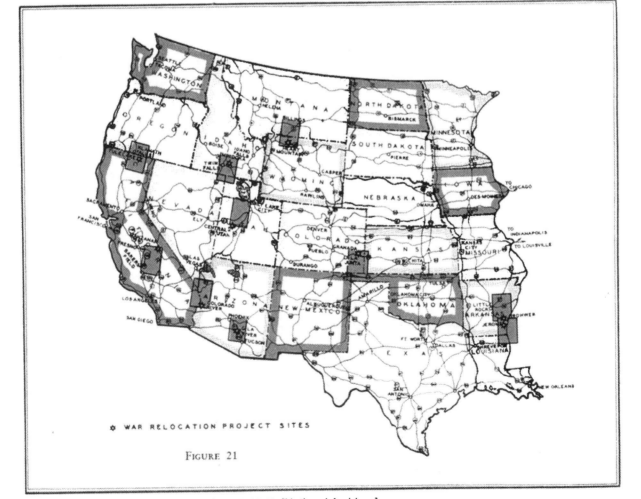

☼ WAR RELOCATION PROJECT SITES

FIGURE 21

Document 34. Map, Relocation Project Sites, June 5, 1943. [National Archives]

Supreme Court of the United States

No. 22 ——— , *October Term, 19*44

Fred Toyosaburo Korematsu,

> Petitioner,

vs.

The United States of America.

On writ of Certiorari to *the United States Circuit Court of Appeals for the* Ninth ———— *Circuit.*

This cause *came on to be heard on the transcript of the record from the United States Circuit Court of Appeals for the* Ninth ———— *Circuit, and was argued by counsel.*

On consideration whereof, *It is ordered* and adjudged ——— ——————————————————— *by this Court that the* judgment ——————— *of the said United States Circuit Court of Appeals, in this cause, be, and the same is hereby,* affirmed; ——— ————————————; *and that this cause be, and the same is hereby, remanded to the* District ——— *Court of the United States for the* Northern ——— *District of* California.

> Per Mr. Justice Black,
> December 18, 1944.

Concurring opinion by Mr. Justice Frankfurter.

Dissenting opinion by Mr. Justice Jackson.

Dissenting opinion by Mr. Justice Murphy.

Dissenting opinion by Mr. Justice Roberts.

Presbytery of the Redwoods

PETITION TO THE CONGRESS OF THE UNITED STATES OF AMERICA

The Presbytery of The Redwoods, meeting in executive session at San Anselmo, California, April 15, 1942, hereby petitions Congress to give consideration to the problem of Japanese citizens and aliens in this Coastal Area. While fully recognizing the need for authorities to take all measures necessary to insure defense of our shores from hostile attack from without, and subversive activity within, we feel that the policy of total evacuation is unnecessarily drastic and severe. We call attention to the following considerations:

1. The waiving of constitutional rights of minority groups of citizens without due process of law opens the way to persecution of other minority groups, thereby fostering disunity and imperiling the safety of our country.

2. We strongly urge that hearings be held in various evacuation centers with a view to ascertaining the loyalty of American citizens, in order that they may return to their homes and useful work as soon as possible.

3. Our treatment of the Japanese here furnishes ammunition for Japanese propaganda chiefs in their role as champion of the colored races.

4. Our treatment of Japanese in America will most certainly be reflected in the treatment of Americans in Japan, and occupied lands.

5. Caucasian church workers should be allowed to continue their work among evacuees in order to continue Americanization and sustain morale.

RECEIVED
APR 25 1942
HQ. WDC and
4th ARMY

Attest

THE PRESBYTERY OF THE REDWOODS

BY: _____
Stated Clerk

San Anselmo, California
April 15, 1942

Document 36. Petition requesting reconsideration of Japanese-American evacuation, April 15, 1942. [National Archives]

Today And Tomorrow

By Walter Lippmann

The Fifth Column On The Coast

SAN FRANCISCO.—The enemy alien problem on the Pacific Coast, or much more accurately the Fifth Column problem, is very serious and it is very special. What makes it so serious and so special is that the Pacific Coast is in imminent danger of a combined attack from within and from without. **LIPPMANN** The danger is not, as it would be in the inland centers or perhaps even for the present on the Atlantic Coast, from sabotage alone. The peculiar danger of the Pacific Coast is in a Japanese raid accompanied by enemy action inside American territory.

This combination can be very formidable indeed. For while the striking power of Japan from the sea and air might not in itself be overwhelming at any one point just now, Japan could strike a blow which might do irreparable damage if it were accompanied by the kind of organized sabotage to which this part of the country is specially vulnerable.

This is a sober statement of the situation, in fact a report, based not on speculation but on what is known to have taken place and to be taking place in this area of the war. It is a fact that the Japanese navy has been reconnoitering the Pacific Coast more or less continually and for a considerable period of time, testing and feeling out the American defenses. It is a fact that communication takes place between the enemy at sea and enemy agents on land.

These are facts which we shall ignore or minimize at our peril. It is also a fact that since the outbreak of the Japanese war there has been no important sabotage on the Pacific Coast. From what we know about Hawaii and about the Fifth Column in Europe this is not, as some have liked to think, a sign that there is nothing to be feared. It is a sign that the blow is well-organized and that it is held back until it can be struck with maximum effect.

IN PREPARING TO REPEL the attack the Army and Navy have all the responsibility but they are facing it with one hand tied down in Washington. I am sure I understand fully and appreciate thoroughly the unwillingness of Washington to adopt a policy of mass evacuation and mass internment of all those who are technically enemy aliens. But I submit that Washington is not defining the problem on the Pacific Coast correctly and that therefore it is raising insoluble issues unnecessarily and failing to deal with the practical issues promptly. No one ever can hope to get the right answer unless he first asks the right questions.

The official approach to the danger is through a series of unrealities. There is the assumption that it is a problem of "enemy aliens." As a matter of fact it is certainly also a problem of native-born American citizens. There is the assumption that a citizen may not be interfered with unless he has committed an overt act, or at least unless there is strong evidence that he is about to commit an overt act.

There is the assumption that if the rights of a citizen are abridged anywhere, they have been abridged everywhere. The effect of these assumptions has been to precipitate legalistic and ideological arguments between the military authorities out here and the civil authorities in Washington, and between the aroused citizenry of the coast and their fellow-countrymen in the interior.

A MUCH SIMPLER approach will, I believe, yield much more practical results. Forget for a moment all about enemy aliens, dual citizenship, naturalized citizens, native citizens of enemy alien parentage, and consider a warship in San Francisco harbor, an airplane plant in Los Angeles, a general's headquarters at Oshkosh, and an admiral's at Podunk. Then think of the lineal descendant, if there happened to be such a person, of George Washington, the father of his country, and consider what happens to Mr. Washington if he decides he would like to visit the warship, or take a walk in the airplane plant, or to drop in and photograph the general and the admiral in their quarters.

He is stopped by the sentry. He has to prove who he is. He has to prove that he has a good reason for doing what he wishes to do. He has to register, sign papers, and wear an identification button. Then perhaps, if he proves his case, he is escorted by an armed guard while he does his errand, and until he has been checked out of the place and his papers and his button have been returned. Have Mr. Washington's constitutional rights been abridged?

Has he been denied the dignity of the human person? Has his loyalty been impugned?

NOW IT SEEMS to me that this is in principle and in general the procedure which ought to be used for all persons in a zone which the military authorities regard as open to enemy attack. In that zone, as in the corridors of the general's headquarters or on the deck of the warship or within the gates of the airplane plant, everyone should be compelled to prove that he has a good reason for being there, and no one should be allowed to come and go until he has proved that his business is necessary and consistent with the national defense.

In the vital and vulnerable areas it should be the rule that residence, employment, communication by telephone, telegraph, automobile and railroad are confined to licensed persons who are fully identified and whose activities are fully known to the authorities and to their neighbors. The Pacific Coast is officially a combat zone: Some part of it may at any moment be a battlefield. Nobody's constitutional rights include the right to reside and do business on a battlefield. And nobody ought to be on a battlefield who has no good reason for being there. There is plenty of room elsewhere for him to exercise his rights.

THIS IS IN SUBSTANCE the system of policing which necessarily prevails in a war zone. By this system the constitutional and international questions about aliens and citizens do not arise at the very place where they confuse the issues and prevent the taking of thorough measures of security. Under this system all persons are in principle treated alike. As a matter of national policy there is no discrimination. But at the same time the authorities on the spot in the threatened region are able to act decisively, and let the explanations and the reparations come later.

This approach to the question by-passes the problem which, as I see it, has caused the trouble in Washington. For what Washington has been trying to find is a policy for dealing with all enemy aliens everywhere and all potential Fifth Columnists everywhere. Yet a policy which may be wise in most parts of the country may be extremely fool-hardy in a combat zone.

Therefore, much the best thing to do is to recognize the Western combat zone as territory quite different from the rest of the country, and then to set up in that zone a special regime. This has been done on the Bataan Peninsula, in Hawaii, in Alaska, in the Canal Zone. Why not also on the threatened West Coast of the United States?

Document 37. Newspaper column, "The Fifth Column On The Coast," by Walter Lippmann, February 12, 1942. [National Archives]

The Fence By an Evacuee

"The barbed wire fences are to keep cattle outside." a man who was eating at my side in a mess hall said. "So I would not sign the petition to Washington".

But most everybodyelse signed the petition asking no fence be erected around the center. There appeared at that time in the Sentinel a strong editorial condemning the fence. The petition was forwarded to Washington. No answer. No explanation by our WRA officials either. The barbed wire fence was erected in spite of such a protest -- without any explanation. Yet some kept on believing the fence was to keep the cattle out, until they saw watch towers being built and soldiers in them. Then even their creditity was dashed to pieced.

"Why these fences when we never think of leaving the center?" some asked.

When the evacuees were moved from Pomona Assembly Center and from the one at Santa Anita where their freedom was nil, they were made to believe that at the Relocation Center which is located outside of the western military zone their freedom of action will be mostly restored. So their diappointment was indeed acute when they first found out that they could not go to the towns of Cody and Powell even for shopping, then saw the barbed wire fences going up and the watch towers at strategic places built.

Document 38a. Essay, "The Fence," by an evacuee, August 11, 1943. [National Archives]

99 out of 100 wondered "Why all these restrictions." Then resentment followed.

I think the above took place in November some time 1942. Then one day, a group of women crept outside of the fence on the southern side and venured to the dump yard to pick up old wires to use them for artificial flower making. (They could not buy wires at the stores. The Heart Mountain center having been opened in a desert that had been bare of any junk piles, wires or any metalic materials. Artificial flower making was at its height and there were about 3 intructors to teack women flok the art.) Well, these few women were busy in picking wires from old lettuce crates etc. when suddenly a jeep approached and M. P. put them in it and took them to the guard house and they were kept there some time (some say over night, I do not know whether it was so). People were indignant.

One day a group of children, some of whom were a young as four years old, approached the watch tower (in broad daylight) at the north-western corner of the center and passed it a few steps and were indulged in playing there. After several whistle blowing to caution the children to trace back inside the tower which they apparently did not understand, M. P. came and hustled the children in a jeep and took them to the guard house and kept them there until Mr Robertson came and rescued them (I think our block chairman reported the incident to a block meeting).

Then a shooting of an evacuee by a M. P. at Topaz was reported in newspapers because the evacuee approached the wire fence too closely. Then it dawned on even very credulous souls that the

Document 38b. Essay, "The Fence," by an evacuee, August 11, 1943. [National Archives]

army meant business when they set up the fence. When young children go too close the fence, mothers would shout at the top of their voice "Don't go there. Come back".

Sometime in February 1943 Mr. Barber, the former Community Service Dept. Head, came to visit our center. (He works in the Washington WRA office). Surrounding him, we -- block chairmen and a few leaders -- had a tea party. Everyone asked Mr. Barber one and the same question: "Why this restriction? At Amache relocation center, evacuees could go to a neighboring twon very freely. Why the same freedom not given to us in H. M.?" "Well," Mr. Barber answered "someone inCody overheard a couple men were saying 'if I see a Jap in the town, I will shoot and kill him". "We are cautious. Hence this restriction etc."

Late in May the Victory Garden on the western side of the center was opened. Then Mr. Todd announced that Victory gardeners could stay outside the fence till sundown. Everyone was eager to take advantage of the extended time limit and went out in evenings. The towers around the center are now empty until about nine o'clock P. M. Guards in day time were removed to outer towers. Now people seem to have forgotten that the wire fences still stand. They do not seem to mind. The fences are lost from gossiping lips.

A few Japanese-Americans visited this center the other day. They said "these watch towers are bad. The relocation centers at Poston and Gila have no fences even. What are these menacing guard towers for?"

In going to Cody and Powell, evacuees will be questioned by M. P. and must show passes. As far as the evacuees are concerned, this procedure is not very humiliating to comply with. But American people passing on the scene come to think of the evacuees more and more in the terms of internees. No wonder that the city councils of Cody and Powell have passed the resolutions limiting our visiting of their cities. The fact evacuees are under the glaring lights of watch towers and they are questioned by M. P. every time they go out of the camp must make outsiders think we are internees. There is no question of this interfering with the relocation of the evacuees, because people outside think we are dangerous characters. This interfers with the carrying out of the main purpose of the Relocation Center -- relocation.

I am one of the residents and am familiar with psychological movements of the fellow residents. And I think there will be no trouble inside the center in future big enough to need the presence of military police. Let Japanese police assume all the responsibility the military police is now functioning. It will remove the stigma of concentration camp from our relocation center. It will relieve many soldiers from here to an active service. Neighboring towns would open their doors wide for the evacuees.

If Japanese-American boys are good to serve the U. S. army, (and they are) they should be good enough to assume the duty of police works in the WRA camp. (my opinion).

Inconnection with this assumption of duties by the Nisei, I want to say further -- that all the important duties now assumed

by the Administrative officers (Caucasian), should be transferred to the Niseis (except the positions of the project
directors and a few others).   The evacuees are criticised for
bering irresponsible, negligent, and not quite honest in dis-
charinging their duties in the center.   Why?   because we
evacuees are dependent on the Government.   Our psychology is
"Let our Uncle Sam do it".   Way down in our psychology is that
consciousness that injustice was done to the Japanese-Americans
in evacuation and relocation.   That is perhaps the reason why
boys on the Agricultural project is not efficient.   Carpenters
and plumbers are not efficient.   Now Caucasian supervisors
assume responsibilities for their being inefficient.

The center will be better in every respect.

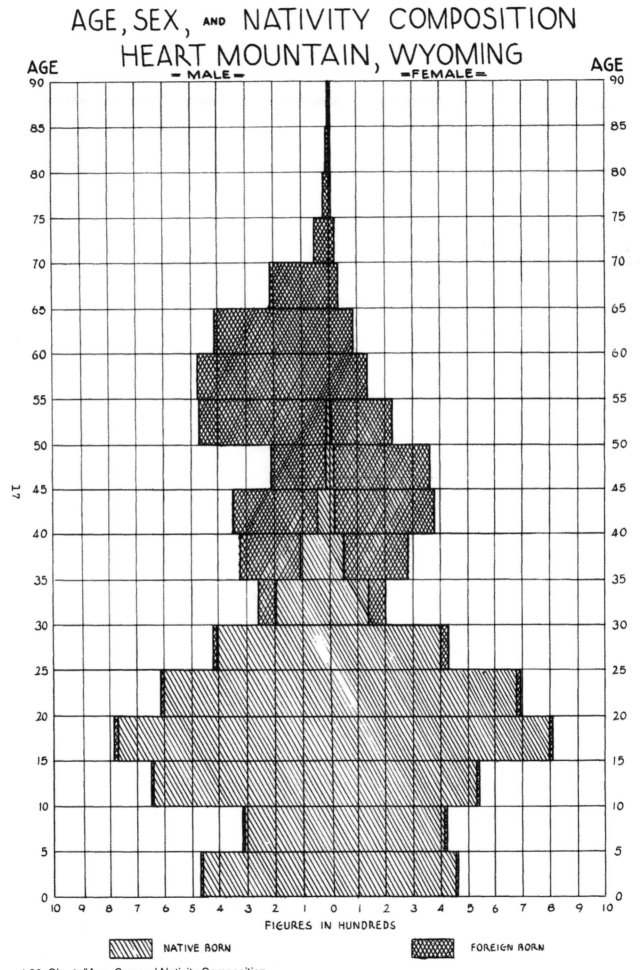

AGE, SEX, AND NATIVITY COMPOSITION
HEART MOUNTAIN, WYOMING

—MALE— =FEMALE=

FIGURES IN HUNDREDS

NATIVE BORN   FOREIGN BORN

Document 39. Chart, "Age, Sex and Nativity Composition, Heart Mountain, Wyoming," November 1942. [National Archives]

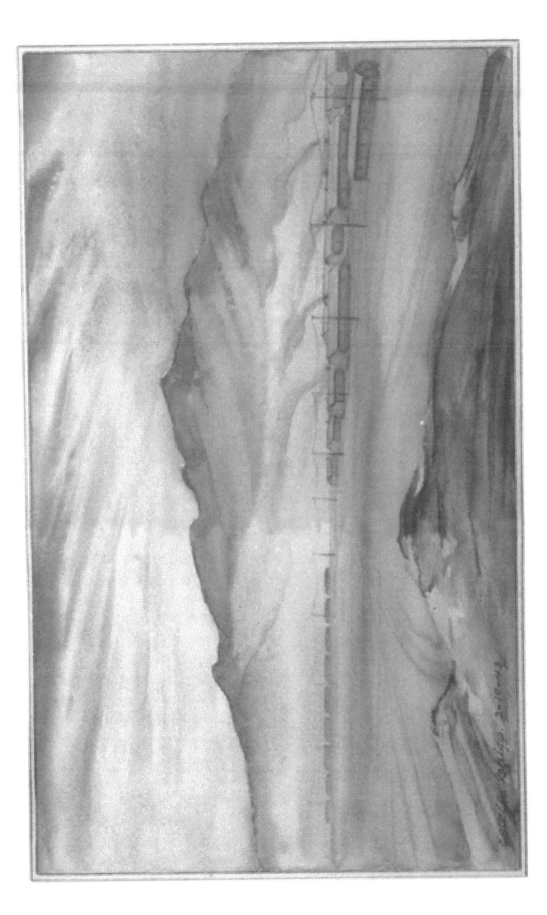

Document 40. Watercolor of Heart Mountain by Estelle Ishigo, February 19, 1943. [National Archives]

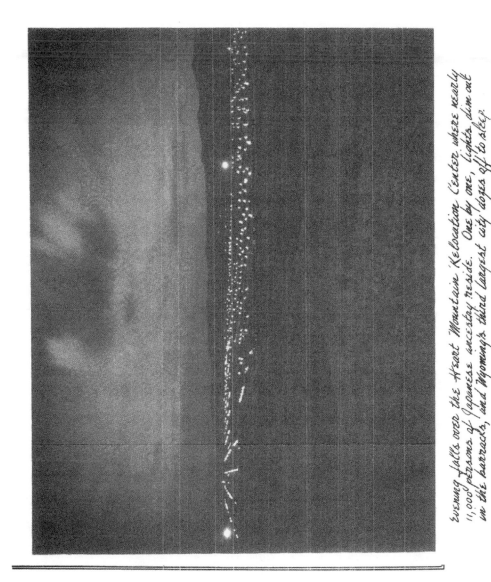

Evening falls over the Heart Mountain Relocation Center, where nearly 11,000 persons of Japanese ancestry reside. One by one, lights dim out in the barracks, and Wyoming's third largest city dozes off to sleep.

Document 41. Photograph, "Heart Mountain," November 1942. [National Archives]

VOLUME 1 NO. 4

JULY 7, 1943

HEART MOUNTAIN BUDDHIST CHURCH WEEKLY JOURNAL

O'BON COMMEMORATION JULY 10-11

SIGNIFICANCE OF O-BON

O-Bon services have been in practice ever since the time of Gotama Buddha, six centuries before the birth of Christ. Originating in India, the custom passed on into China in the year 538 A.D., the time of the Wu Emperor of Liang. And in the third year of Saimei which is 657 A.D. in our calendar, it was first observed in Japan.

The word O-Bon is derived from the Japanese and Chinese word "Uranbon" or "Urabon" which is Ullambana in original Sanskrit. The Urabon is the correct term for the service, but in its long history the first syllable was discarded and it became just simply "Bon". "O" was applied as an honorific. Thus, today we have the word "O-Bon." Ullambana means to hang upside down. Mogallana's mother was hanging up-side down and was suffering and she was saved by her son's deep piety and the teaching of Buddha. Bon is a tray or bowl. It is an article in which foods or gifts are carried. So "O-Bon" means to carry foods or gifts and give to others.

There is a four-fold significance in the O-Bon service. Namely the spirit of giving, the feeling of peace and harmony, the expression of gratitude and the thought of parental piety. The O-Bon was first started by Mogallana, one of the ten great deciples of Buddha. He was always very thoughtful of his mother. Then he learned that she was suffering in the hell of greediness because of her past selfish deeds. He was very much concerned and attempted to save her, but it was beyond his power. He went to Buddha for advice. Buddha told him to invite noble teachers and friends and perform a service and to give a feast to all after the service. He did as he was told. His mother listened to the words of the noble teachers and realized for the first time the right way of living and the happy and harmonious friendship created through the spirit of giving at the feast and enabled her to overcome her selfish greediness. Mogallana was so overjoyed when he saw his mother saved at last that he found himself dancing. Soon everybody joined him. The feast ended with a happy and harmonious dance. This is the origin of Bon Odori.

On O-Bon we hold a memorial service to pay our respect to our beloved ones and to express our gratitude to our ancestors to whom we owe our existence. The observance of O-Bon refreshes our minds to live a more harmonious and peaceful life at home and in the community through its spirit of giving and Bon Odori. It also reminds us that the origin of any kind of suffering has its roots in selfishness. And the selfishness is overcome only by the spirit of giving as it did for Mogallana's mother. Buddha teaches that giving is the prime importance to salvation.

Therefore, it has become a custom and tradition in Japan that in the O-Bon season gifts are given to friends and relatives. Thus we encourage the spirit of giving through which we can live a more intimate and harmonious life.

FACTS ON BUDDHIST CHURCH

Being of non-sectarian organization, an interesting fact was revealed on the Heart Mt. Buddhist Community Church.

Represented by all Buddhist sects adhering to the teachings of Shakyamuni Buddha, it reveals a composited picture of an org-

O'BON SERVICE PROGRAM

Sat. July 10
2:00 P.M. Service at the cemetry
6:30 P.M. Evening Service 17-25
7:30 P.M. Bon Odori at Block 17 vacant lot

Sun. July 11
9:00 A.M. Sunday School 17-25, 14-25, 24-26
10:30 A.M. Young People's Service 17-25
2:00 P.M. General O-Bon Service 17-25

S. S. TEACHERS ASSOCIATION

Officers were selected at a recent meeting of the newly organized Sunday School Teachers Association of the Heart Mt. Buddhist Church. Those chosen were Hiromi Inouye, president; Fred Yonemoto, vice president; Yuri Taniguchi, Japanese secretary; Mitsuye Kodama, English secretary; Helen Munekiyo, corresponding secretary; Shizu Takeuchi, treasurer. Inouye and Yonemoto will also head the research department, and on the publications committee are Rev. Yoshikami, George Tanaka, Tatsuo Sakamoto, Asako Kubo and Yonemoto.

anization welded together of former individual churches from Oregon, Washington, and California.

With a board member of 200, it is represented by all Buddhist sects, with a predominance of Nishi Hongwanji members. Other churches represented are Higashi, Jodo, Zen, Nichiren, Daishi, and Buddhist Brotherhood of America.

It is a representative overall community organization.

All persons interested in Buddhism are cordially welcome to the services.
——— o O o ———

ASSOCIATED STUDENTS OF HUNT

Reyko Miura
Hist.

Katsumi Okamoto
Pub. Mgr.

Mrs. M. Pollock
Adviser

Mr. M. Barber
Adviser

Student

Calvin Ninomiya
Pres.

Shig Sakamoto
Vice-Pres.

Katherine Matsuda
Cor.-Sec.

Sue Kawasaki
Rec.-Sec.

Dutch Watanabe
Treas.

Council

Real democracy is not hereditary. It is a way of living. Although the home and community have a great deal of influence on the citizen of tomorrow, the school also plays an important roll. The school, through which the Student Council, gives us a vehicle through which we can practice the principles of democratic government. The Student Council, based upon student body representation, gives the youth a chance to think out the problems that affect his school life. During the school year, many problems have arisen that have challenged the abilities of the council, but the students have more than shown their ability to solve student-government problems. Accomplishing much, they have provided the year with many colorful events to remember and recall.

STUDENT COUNCIL IN ACTION

FIRST ROW—Nagamatsu, Kenao; Kurasaka, Roland; Sugimoto, Martha; Oye, Ikuko; Suzuki, Fumiko; Nakamura, Eileen; Yasunobu, Bobby; Kato, Zealchi.

SECOND ROW—Haga, Aiko; Suzuki, Jimmy; Tazuma, Jimmy; Zaloji, Hideo; Machida, Calvin; Fujino, Mitzi.
THIRD ROW—Uyeki, Eugene; Matsushima, John; Sakamoto, Shig; Kaneko, Harry; Nakagawa, Bunzo.

INTERVIEW WITH THE STUDENT RELOCATION COUNSELOR

The counselor showed that there is a marked decline in the number of applicants for student relocation. She gave several reasons for this decline:

(1) It might be too early for application inasmuch as the term has yet six weeks to go.

(2) Up to now there were many high school graduates who since evacuation were planning to go out to school. Most of them, if not all of them, have succeeded in carrying out their plans. No longer is there a back-log of students requiring counseling. After a graduating class starts making plans there is an increase in the number of applicants for student aid.

(3) The counselor believes there is a let down in interest in higher education because there is a lack of student guidance in the high school.

(4) The accelerated drafting of young fellows might be playing an important part in discouraging them to consider higher education.

(5) The very few outstanding students are looking ahead for as much education as they possibly can receive beofre being drafted.

(6) Among the girls the number of applicants have fallen way down. However, ther has been an increase in the number of girls interested in the Cadet Nursing Corps Training. Due to bottlenecks of one kind or another many girls are finding the delay very discouraging. The chances for acceptance is a little more encouraging if the applicant applies in person. As a result this office is becoming of less and less help to them. We have some information on the matter but as yet we have been unable to place any girl in training.

In discussing the caliber of students desiring help from our office, we find most of them have definite plans. That is, they want to become doctors, engineers, chemists, laboratory technicians, nurses, etc. I think they are the top students. It is unfortunate but true that this type of student is the hardest to place in the better schools. They are required to get a Provost Marshall clearance before they can register at such inexpensive and professionally desirable schools such as U. of Minnesota, Michigan, Ohio, Wisconsin, Western Michigan, Nebraska, etc. The private schools are expensive or else do not have the desired curriculum.

I'm glad they are doing something about the student aid fund. I think the announcement will encourage many of the borderline students who have been worrying about meeting their tuition. Since the goal is to help 50 students I'm sure students who thought they couldn't rate a scholarship will be encouraged to further their education.

I think the teachers should encourage the students to continue their education. The future should not be made to look hopeless and discouraging. Very few teachers take the time to find out what the NSRC (National Student Relocation Council) is doing. Because of this lack of information individual teachers are unable to act as personal counselors to students whose confidence they have won. In particular, there are two kinds of teachers. One group have come here because it's a paying job. The other are teachers who are interested in the problem that evacuation has given birth. The former group have no intentions of going out of their way to help the students in their dilemma. Unfortunately this group predominates in the Topaz High School faculty. To cite an example I've tried to interest the faculty in starting the student aid fund over two and a half months ago when I received notice from the headquarters of the NSRC that the NSRC funds were very low. The matter has been kicked around until finally the students themselves have taken the initiative to raise the funds. Unless more teachers take interest in the students and their problems we will find that the high school aged children are destined to be the problem children of the future. One outstanding teacher of the appointive staff told K.O. that if he wanted to see a better school at Topaz, he might as well relocate and complete his high school education on the outside because as far as she was concerned the WRA cannot improve upon the present educational system here at Topaz. We can appreciate her frankness. On the other hand it shows the defeatist attitude which is prevalent among the faculty. Knowing the hopelessness of the situation no effort is made to correct the glaring faults. Doing a bad job from day to day will not give the Nisei the education they are going to require to fight the second fight after the war of totalitarianism on foreign soil is won--that fight is going to be the battle against intolerance at home. Perhaps your department can help in some way to encourage the WRA to look at the long view problem and cope with it more vigorously. It seem the WRA is not too concerned because the students have been telling me the best teachers have been discharged, used in the wrong departments, and lately transferred. Several students have been complaining about the calibre of teachers. I'm willing to give anyone the benefit of the doubt but when so many students seem to agree on the same points I feel the stories are not just made up to agitate. Under the circumstances these criticisms should be investigated and see to it that, if true, they don't happen over and over again. One appointive staff faculty member has mentioned to me that in her opinion some of the teachers have no business being here. She mentioned names.

As you know, this section deals with delinquency also. We are dealing with a problem child, and every effort we make to set him straight, certain members of the appointive staff do a fine job of undoing our efforts. They take him to Delta, keep him up late playing cards, go with him to dances, baby him, and in every way maek it impossible for him to stand on his two feet. He owes money to faculty members, students and neighbors. I don't see how he is going to pay his debts. The residents are wise to him now and leave hin alone. Now we must educate the appointive staff, the very people who should be working with us and not against us in teaching him how to grow up. If they mean well by him, effort would be made to make a man out of him and not let him have his own way all the time.

The draft no doubt has discouraged many young fellows from continuing with their education. However, T.O. had a stimulating affect upon students when he returned from Michigan after one semesters work at that University. He was drafted so came to Topaz to visit his mother. During his short stay here he spoke to several core classes. He told the students not to give up on their plans for going to college. He's glad he was able to go to college for even one semester. The environment, the college life, the students he met, the encouragement professors gave him, the general feeling of getting ahead are now in his veins. He knows how grand it is to go to college. When the war is over his one goal is to complete his college training. T.O. told the students that unless you get a taste of what it is like, it is going to be difficult to make up your mind to go to college when you are much older than the average student. It's like a drug. You want more of it once you know the feel.. He emphasized--get as much education as you possibly can before you are called to service. You'll never regret it. Do you know T.O. was a Buddhist? When he went to Michigan he attended church every Sunday and the Y.P. group at night. He doesn't understand Christianity yet but he says the people make you want to go back every Sunday. He seems to have been impressed by the treatment he received by the young people at a particular church near the campus. He told me, "they even help you put on your overcoat." He's soft hearted so I imagine the small favors impressed him very much. Shortly I will find out how effective his message to the students was. I hope more and more students take T.O.'s advice and go as far as they can in their education. Along this line I think the faculty can be of inestimable value.

I think the PTA if well organized and well led, can be a strong means to make the parents' wishes known. Perhaps it is too much to ask the parents, especially the Issei, to assume such a role when their background has not prepared them for active work for them. No doubt they would support any group who will take the active role. On the other hand the school system has not yet effected a successful way in which to bridge the gap between the school and parent. In other words there seems to be too little communication between the school and the parents. In order to keep the parents interested in the school system a closer association must be maintained. The parents never have had to question the policy or interfere with the school system. Therefore, unless the parents are brought more closely in contact with the teachers and school system the desired parent-teacher-school association will be difficult to achieve. Here the sincerity of the faculty in the problem is of vital importance. Of course we cannot underestimate the language handicap. Underneath it all this barrier might be the real fly in the ointment. Unless the teacher is sincerely interested in the welfare of the students she won't take the time to patiently explain the students needs with the parents.

Hasn't the Community Council an education committee? I think it is generally agreed that something has to be done to improve the school system here at Topaz. Talking about it won't solve the problem. The council committee should be used to look into the matter and suggest improvements. At least, the committee could publish their findings so that the concerned, indifferent, and don't know groups of parents will become familiar with what is going on and take active interest in the welfare of the students. Undoubtedly there is much room for improvement on the part of student behavior. If cooperation can be achieved among the students, faculty and parents the hoped for improvement might be forthcoming. If active interest is taken in the educational system by the community as a whole I'm sure the authorities would be willing to cooperate. And too the faculty will be required to be on their toes conscious of the fact that they are being carefully and critically observed.

"The growing movement of peaceful mass demonstrations by Negroes is something new in the South, something understandable.... Let Congress heed their rising voices, for they will be heard."

—New York Times editorial
Saturday, March 19, 1960

Heed Their Rising Voices

As the whole world knows by now, thousands of Southern Negro students are engaged in widespread non-violent demonstrations in positive affirmation of the right to live in human dignity as guaranteed by the U. S. Constitution and the Bill of Rights. In their efforts to uphold these guarantees, they are being met by an unprecedented wave of terror by those who would deny and negate that document which the whole world looks upon as setting the pattern for modern freedom....

In Orangeburg, South Carolina, when 400 students peacefully sought to buy doughnuts and coffee at lunch counters in the business district, they were forcibly ejected, tear-gassed, soaked to the skin in freezing weather with fire hoses, arrested en masse and herded into an open barbed-wire stockade to stand for hours in the bitter cold.

In Montgomery, Alabama, after students sang "My Country, 'Tis of Thee" on the State Capitol steps, their leaders were expelled from school, and truckloads of police armed with shotguns and tear-gas ringed the Alabama State College Campus. When the entire student body protested to state authorities by refusing to re-register, their dining hall was padlocked in an attempt to starve them into submission.

In Tallahassee, Atlanta, Nashville, Savannah, Greensboro, Memphis, Richmond, Charlotte, and a host of other cities in the South, young American teenagers, in face of the entire weight of official state apparatus and police power, have boldly stepped forth as protagonists of democracy. Their courage and amazing restraint have inspired millions and given a new dignity to the cause of freedom.

Small wonder that the Southern violators of the Constitution fear this new, non-violent brand of freedom fighter ... even as they fear the upswelling right-to-vote movement. Small wonder that they are determined to destroy the one man who, more than any other, symbolizes the new spirit now sweeping the South—the Rev. Dr. Martin Luther King, Jr., world-famous leader of the Montgomery Bus Protest. For it is his doctrine of non-violence which has inspired and guided the students in their widening wave of sit-ins; and it this same Dr. King who founded and is president of the Southern Christian Leadership Conference—the organization which is spearheading the surging right-to-vote movement. Under Dr. King's direction the Leadership Conference conducts Student Workshops and Seminars in the philosophy and technique of non-violent resistance.

Again and again the Southern violators have answered Dr. King's peaceful protests with intimidation and violence. They have bombed his home almost killing his wife and child. They have assaulted his person. They have arrested him seven times—for "speeding," "loitering" and similar "offenses." And now they have charged him with "perjury"—a *felony* under which they could imprison him for *ten years.* Obviously, their real purpose is to remove him physically as the leader to whom the students and millions of others—look for guidance and support, and thereby to intimidate *all* leaders who may rise in the South. Their strategy is to behead this affirmative movement, and thus to demoralize Negro Americans and weaken their will to struggle. The defense of Martin Luther King, spiritual leader of the student sit-in movement, clearly, therefore, is an integral part of the total struggle for freedom in the South.

Decent-minded Americans cannot help but applaud the creative daring of the students and the quiet heroism of Dr. King. But this is one of those moments in the stormy history of Freedom when men and women of good will must do more than applaud the rising-to-glory of others. The America whose good name hangs in the balance before a watchful world, the America whose heritage of Liberty these Southern Upholders of the Constitution are defending, is *our* America as well as theirs ...

We must heed their rising voices—yes—but we must add our own.

We must extend ourselves above and beyond moral support and render the material help so urgently needed by those who are taking the risks, facing jail, and even death in a glorious re-affirmation of our Constitution and its Bill of Rights.

We urge you to join hands with our fellow Americans in the South by supporting, with your dollars, this Combined Appeal for all three needs—the defense of Martin Luther King—the support of the embattled students—and the struggle for the right-to-vote.

Your Help Is Urgently Needed . . . NOW!!

Stella Adler
Raymond Pace Alexander
Harry Van Arsdale
Harry Belafonte
Julie Belafonte
Dr. Algernon Black
Marc Blitzstein
William Branch
Marlon Brando
Mrs. Ralph Bunche
Diahann Carroll

Dr. Alan Knight Chalmers
Richard Coe
Nat King Cole
Cheryl Crawford
Dorothy Dandridge
Ossie Davis
Sammy Davis, Jr.
Ruby Dee
Dr. Philip Elliott
Dr. Harry Emerson Fosdick

Anthony Franciosa
Lorraine Hansberry
Rev. Donald Harrington
Nat Hentoff
James Hicks
Mary Hinkson
Van Heflin
Langston Hughes
Morris Iushewitz
Mahalia Jackson
Mordecai Johnson

John Killens
Eartha Kitt
Rabbi Edward Klein
Hope Lange
John Lewis
Viveca Lindfors
Carl Murphy
Don Murray
John Murray
A. J. Muste
Frederick O'Neal

L. Joseph Overton
Clarence Pickett
Shad Polier
Sidney Poitier
A. Philip Randolph
John Raitt
Elmer Rice
Jackie Robinson
Mrs. Eleanor Roosevelt
Bayard Rustin
Robert Ryan

Maureen Stapleton
Frank Silvera
Hope Stevens
George Tabori
Rev. Gardner C. Taylor
Norman Thomas
Kenneth Tynan
Charles White
Shelley Winters
Max Youngstein

We in the south who are struggling daily for dignity and freedom warmly endorse this appeal

Rev. Ralph D. Abernathy
(Montgomery, Ala.)

Rev. Fred L. Shuttlesworth
(Birmingham, Ala.)

Rev. Kelley Miller Smith
(Nashville, Tenn.)

Rev. W. A. Dennis
(Chattanooga, Tenn.)

Rev. C. K. Steele
(Tallahassee, Fla.)

Rev. Matthew D. McCollom
(Orangeburg, S. C.)

Rev. William Holmes Borders
(Atlanta, Ga.)

Rev. Douglas Moore
(Durham, N. C.)

Rev. Wyatt Tee Walker
(Petersburg, Va.)

Rev. Walter L. Hamilton
(Norfolk, Va.)

I. S. Levy
(Columbia, S. C.)

Rev. Martin Luther King, Sr.
(Atlanta, Ga.)

Rev. Henry C. Bunton
(Memphis, Tenn.)

Rev. S. S. Seay, Sr.
(Montgomery, Ala.)

Rev. Samuel W. Williams
(Atlanta, Ga.)

Rev. A. L. Davis
(New Orleans, La.)

Mrs. Katie E. Whickham
(New Orleans, La.)

Rev. W. H. Hall
(Hattiesburg, Miss.)

Rev. J. E. Lowery
(Mobile, Ala.)

Rev. T. J. Jemison
(Baton Rouge, La.)

Please mail this coupon TODAY!

Committee To Defend Martin Luther King
and
The Struggle For Freedom In The South
312 West 125th Street, New York 27, N. Y.
UNiversity 6-1700

I am enclosing my contribution of $_____
for the work of the Committee.

Name_____
(PLEASE PRINT)

Address_____

City_____　　Zone____　State____

☐ I want to help　　☐ Please send further information

Please make checks payable to:
Committee To Defend Martin Luther King

COMMITTEE TO DEFEND MARTIN LUTHER KING AND THE STRUGGLE FOR FREEDOM IN THE SOUTH
312 West 125th Street, New York 27, N. Y. UNiversity 6-1700

Chairmen: A. Philip Randolph, Dr. Gardner C. Taylor; *Chairmen of Cultural Division:* Harry Belafonte, Sidney Poitier; *Treasurer:* Nat King Cole; *Executive Director:* Bayard Rustin; *Chairmen of Church Division:* Father George B. Ford, Rev. Harry Emerson Fosdick, Rev. Thomas Kilgore, Jr., Rabbi Edward E. Klein; *Chairman of Labor Division:* Morris Iushewitz

Document 45. Advertisement, "Heed Their Rising Voices," March 29, 1960. [National Archives]

89TH CONGRESS
1ST SESSION

S. 1160

[Report No. 813]

IN THE SENATE OF THE UNITED STATES

FEBRUARY 17, 1965

Mr. LONG of Missouri (for himself, Mr. ANDERSON, Mr. BARTLETT, Mr. BAYH, Mr. BOGGS, Mr. BURDICK, Mr. CASE, Mr. DIRKSEN, Mr. ERVIN, Mr. FONG, Mr. HART, Mr. METCALF, Mr. MORSE, Mr. MOSS, Mr. NELSON, Mrs. NEUBERGER, Mr. PROXMIRE, Mr. RIBICOFF, Mr. SMATHERS, Mr. SYMINGTON, Mr. TYDINGS, and Mr. YARBOROUGH) introduced the following bill; which was read twice and referred to the Committee on the Judiciary

OCTOBER 4 (legislative day, OCTOBER 1), 1965

Reported by Mr. LONG of Missouri, with amendments

[Omit the part struck through and insert the part printed in italic]

A BILL

To amend section 3 of the Administrative Procedure Act, chapter 324, of the Act of June 11, 1946 (60 Stat. 238), to clarify and protect the right of the public to information, and for other purposes.

1 *Be it enacted by the Senate and House of Representa-*

2 *tives of the United States of America in Congress assembled,*

3 That section 3, chapter 324, of the Act of June 11, 1946

4 (60 Stat. 238), is amended to read as follows:

5 "SEC. 3. Every agency shall make available to the public

6 the following information:

7 "(a) PUBLICATION IN THE FEDERAL REGISTER.—

II

1 Every agency shall separately state and currently publish in

2 the Federal Register for the guidance of the public (A) de-

3 scriptions of its central and field organization and the estab-

4 lished places at which, the officers from whom, and the

5 methods whereby, the public may secure information, make

6 submittals or requests, or obtain decisions; (B) statements

7 of the general course and method by which its functions are

8 channeled and determined, including the nature and require-

9 ments of all formal and informal procedures available; (C)

10 rules of procedure, descriptions of forms available or the

11 places at which forms may be obtained, and instructions as

12 to the scope and contents of all papers, reports, or examina-

13 tions; (D) substantive rules of general applicability adopted

14 as authorized by law, and statements of general policy or in-

15 terpretations of general applicability formulated and adopted

16 by the agency; and (E) every amendment, revision, or

17 repeal of the foregoing. Except to the extent that a person

18 has actual and timely notice of the terms thereof, no person

19 shall in any manner be required to resort to, or be adversely

20 affected by any matter required to be published in the Fed-

21 eral Register and not so published. For purposes of this sub-

22 section, matter which is reasonably available to the class of

23 persons affected thereby shall be deemed published in the

24 Federal Register when incorporated by reference therein

25 with the approval of the Director of the Federal Register.

1 "(b) AGENCY OPINIONS AND ORDERS.—Every agency

2 shall, in accordance with published rules, make available for

3 public inspection and copying (A) all final opinions (in-

4 cluding concurring and dissenting opinions) and all orders

5 made in the adjudication of cases, (B) those statements of

6 policy and interpretations which have been adopted by the

7 agency and are not published in the Federal Register, and

8 (C) *administrative* staff manuals and instructions to staff

9 that affect any member of the public, unless such materials

10 are promptly published and copies offered for sale. To the

11 extent required to prevent a clearly unwarranted invasion of

12 personal privacy, an agency may delete identifying details

13 when it makes available or publishes an opinion, statement

14 of policy, interpretation, or staff manual or instruction: *Pro-*

15 *vided,* That in every case the justification for the deletion

16 must be fully explained in writing. Every agency also shall

17 maintain and make available for public inspection and copy-

18 ing a current index providing identifying information for the

19 public as to any matter which is issued, adopted, or promul-

20 gated after the effective date of this Act and which is re-

21 quired by this subsection to be made available or published.

22 No final order, opinion, statement of policy, interpretation, or

23 staff manual or instruction that affects any member of the

24 public may be relied upon, used or cited as precedent by an

25 agency against any private party unless it has been indexed

1 and either made available or published as provided by this

2 subsection or unless that private party shall have actual

3 and timely notice of the terms thereof.

4 "(c) AGENCY RECORDS.—~~Every~~ *Except with respect*

5 *to the records made available pursuant to subsections (a) and*

6 *(b), every* agency shall, *upon request for identifiable records*

7 *made* in accordance with published rules stating the time,

8 place, *fees to the extent authorized by statute* and procedure

9 to be followed, make ~~all its~~ *such* records promptly available

10 to any person. Upon complaint, the district court of the

11 United States in the district in which the complainant resides,

12 or has his principal place of business, or in which the agency

13 records are situated shall have jurisdiction to enjoin the

14 agency from the withholding of agency records ~~and informa-~~

15 ~~tion~~ and to order the production of any agency records ~~or in-~~

16 ~~formation~~ improperly withheld from the complainant. In

17 such cases the court shall determine the matter de novo and

18 the burden shall be upon the agency to sustain its action. In

19 the event of noncompliance with the court's order, the district

20 court may punish the responsible officers for contempt. Ex-

21 cept as to those causes which the court deems of greater im-

22 portance, proceedings before the district court as authorized

23 by this subsection shall take precedence on the docket over

24 all other causes and shall be assigned for hearing and trial at

25 the earliest practicable date and expedited in every way.

1   "(d) AGENCY PROCEEDINGS.—Every agency having

2 more than one member shall keep a record of the final votes

3 of each member in every agency proceeding and such record

4 shall be available for public inspection.

5   "(e) EXEMPTIONS.—The provisions of this section

6 shall not be applicable to matters that are (1) specifically

7 required by Executive order to be kept secret in the interest

8 of the national defense or foreign policy; (2) related solely

9 to the internal personnel rules and practices of any agency;

10 (3) specifically exempted from disclosure by statute; (4)

11 trade secrets and commercial or financial information ob-

12 tained from ~~the public~~ *any person* and privileged or confi-

13 dential; (5) inter-agency or intra-agency memorandums or

14 letters ~~dealing solely with matters of law or policy~~ *which*

15 *would not be available by law to a private party in litigation*

16 *with the agency*; (6) personnel and medical files and similar

17 files the disclosure of which would constitute a clearly

18 unwarranted invasion of personal privacy; (7) investigatory

19 files compiled for law enforcement purposes except to the

20 extent available by law to a private party; ~~and~~ (8) con-

21 tained in or related to examination, operating, or condition

22 reports prepared by, on behalf of, or for the use of any

23 agency responsible for the regulation or supervision of finan-

24 cial institutions; *and (9) geological and geophysical informa-*

25 *tion and data (including maps) concerning wells.*

1   " (f) LIMITATION OF EXEMPTIONS.—Nothing in this

2   section authorizes withholding of information or limiting

3   the availability of records to the public except as specifically

4   stated in this section, nor shall this section be authority to

5   withhold information from Congress.

6   " (g) PRIVATE PARTY.—As used in this section, 'private

7   party' means any party other than an agency.

8   " (h) EFFECTIVE DATE.—This amendment shall be-

9   come effective one year following the date of the enactment

10   of this Act."

Calendar No. 798

89TH CONGRESS
1ST SESSION

S. 1160

[Report No. 813]

A BILL

To amend section 3 of the Administrative Procedure Act, chapter 324, of the Act of June 11, 1946 (60 Stat. 238), to clarify and protect the right of the public to information, and for other purposes.

By Mr. LONG of Missouri, Mr. ANDERSON, Mr. BARTLETT, Mr. BAYH, Mr. BOGGS, Mr. BURDICK, Mr. CASE, Mr. DIRKSEN, Mr. ERVIN, Mr. FONG, Mr. HART, Mr. METCALF, Mr. MORSE, Mr. MOSS, Mr. NELSON, Mrs. NEUBERGER, Mr. PROXMIRE, Mr. RIBICOFF, Mr. SMATHERS, Mr. SYMINGTON, Mr. TYDINGS, and Mr. YARBOROUGH

FEBRUARY 17, 1965

Read twice and referred to the Committee on the Judiciary.

OCTOBER 4 (legislative day, OCTOBER 1), 1965
Reported with amendments